ELEMENTARY *Greek*

KOINE FOR BEGINNERS

ELEMENTARY *Greek*

KOINE FOR BEGINNERS

YEAR ONE

With Daily Lesson Plans for a 30 week course

by *Christine Gatchell*

Foreword by Gerald R. McDermott

Albuquerque, New Mexico

Published by Open Texture
8200 Montgomery NE No 236
Albuquerque, NM 87109
http://www.opentexture.com

Cover and text design by Susanne Duffner.

Publisher's Cataloging-in-Publication Data

Gatchell, Christine.
    Elementary Greek: Koine for Beginners, Year One / Christine Gatchell ; foreword by Gerald R. McDermott.
        p. cm.
    ISBN 0-9742391-7-8 (pbk)
    1. Bible. N.T. – Language, style – Problems, exercises, etc.   2. Greek language, Biblical – Grammar Problems, exercises, etc.   3. Greek language, Biblical – Self instruction.   I. Title. II. Series.

    PA817.G38   2005   487.4

ISBN   0-9742391-7-8 (Paperback)
ISBN   0-9742391-9-4 (Audio CD)
LCCN   2005930071

Manufactured by Color House Graphics, Inc. Grand Rapids, MI USA
July 2013
Job #40563

TABLE OF *contents*

foreword

I LEARNED GREEK BECAUSE I STUTTERED. IT WAS THE FALL OF 1971 IN NEW YORK City, and I had two other choices as a sophomore at a Jesuit high school: the Modern Language track, which I feared because I could not speak well, and the Science track, for which (I had learned in freshman science) my brain was not wired.

My biggest surprise was that I loved it. Part of the reason was Mr. Marasco, a bachelor layman who came in everyday with an overwhelming enthusiasm for what he called the greatest of all languages. It didn't hurt that Marasco had a flair for the dramatic, proof of which was his winning a Tony award for a Broadway play modeled loosely on our all-boys prep school.

Another reason was the language itself, which had a precision of expression that reminded me of a master mechanic searching for the perfect tool to position a particular piece of metal onto an odd-shaped space. Greek had a similar ability to express every nuance I could possibly think of in my young 14-year-old mind. "Might I" (subjunctive mood) date that girl I saw at the local girls' high school? If so, I sure "hoped to" (optative mood). Most of the time I found that I "was hoping" (imperfect tense) for such a happy outcome, even if I "had failed" (pluperfect tense) often in the past. All of this, and more, was easily put, in classical Greek exactitude.

A third reason was Homer, whose *Iliad* and *Odyssey* we toiled through over the next three years. But the toil hardly felt like work, for the Greek bard's imagination introduced me to an ancient world full of color and drama and heroic virtue. I remember trying to imagine what the "wine-dark sea" looked like; feeling comforted by the goddess Athena's ingenious escapes for her favorite mortal Odysseus and then awed by his courage and fidelity as he battled for twenty-plus years to return to his beloved Penelope. Then there was the *Iliad*, with beautiful Helen, "whose face launched a thousand ships," and the tragic war that was begun with lust and perpetuated by pride.

Then in college, after a spiritual awakening, I started reading Koine (literally, "common," or of the common people) Greek, with an intensity I had never known before. The classical Greek from high school was fun, but this was food for the soul. Providentially, I thought, I was given the Greek language when I had little or no religious feeling. But now I wanted to learn without stopping the primal documents of the community formed by Jesus. I have been reading ever since, almost on a daily basis, and have found New Testament Greek to be the closest thing I have to the mind of Christ.

Koine Greek, the Greek of the New Testament, is not quite as precise as the classical Greek of Homer and Plato. But it comes close. It would not be too much to say that we have a Koine New Testament because of the love for Greek culture which Aristotle and Philip II instilled in Philip's son, Alexander the Great. Alexander's gargantuan conquests brought classical Greek into contact with a host of local languages. As a result of this collision, Greek became the *lingua franca* of the ancient world—even during much of the Roman Empire. Greek took on a new universal quality. This new prestige language of the Greco-Roman world was not the first language for most, or even the language of first choice for many. But it was the language of political, cultural, and economic superiority. If you wanted to communicate with people on the move, you had to learn Koine.

Yet it was not elitist. It was everyday Greek, used in writing wills, friendly and business letters, commercial receipts, and shipping lists. From North Africa opposite Spain, all the way East to Persia in the north and India in the south.

Because it was so important, the only world language of the day, the Jews translated their Hebrew Bible into this Koine. The result was the Septuagint. The first-century Jewish historian Josephus felt compelled to either write his histories in Koine or have them translated into Koine.

Thus it is no surprise that the apostles, most of whom were Jews whose first language was Aramaic, wrote the New Testament in Koine. This was the English of the first century—the world language which everyone who wanted to get ahead knew he had to learn.

Before the twentieth century, many scholars thought Koine was unique to the New Testament, a "Holy Ghost Greek" specially delivered to the apostles for this single collection of writings. But when, after the Second World War, troves of Greek papyri were unearthed, it was discovered that Koine was used throughout the Hellenistic world, particularly for business purposes.

We have also learned that businessmen who caught fish for a living, especially those who lived in Hellenized regions of Galilee, spoke Koine Greek. It was in their best interests, since many of their customers were Romans.

While Jesus' first language was probably Aramaic (the language of the Jews since their return from Babylonian captivity in the 6th century BC), Jesus came from a highly Hellenized area of Galilee. Nazareth, Jesus' hometown, was just a few miles from Sepphoris, a city where Aramaic and Greek were spoken. It was also near Decapolis, a largely Gentile (Greek) city. Jesus' carpentry trade probably brought him to these cities for business.

But it is not only these cultural factors that suggest Jesus spoke Koine Greek. There is also literary evidence in the gospels. His conversations with the Samaritan woman, the Syro-Phoenician woman, and the Roman centurion betray telltale signs of his use of this non-Jewish language.

Which is all the more reason why you should want your children to learn Koine Greek. It is the language through which we have direct access to the words of the little community that has changed the world. That is enough to make anyone want to learn—and it has motivated millions throughout history to pore over these declensions and conjugations, with growing delight.

But there are three more reasons to teach children. First, both linguistics and experience have taught us that children can learn languages far more easily than we adults can. And second, we parents have the opportunity through this series to open doors for our children to both the New Testament and all the Greek classics. And third, learning Koine can be fun for a child. Not only that, but you will know the joy of seeing your child inhabit the words and worlds of ancient peoples.

Gerald R. McDermott
Professor of Religion and Philosophy
Roanoke College

introduction

χαίρειν! (Greetings!) and welcome to Elementary Greek, Year One. These lessons were born out of the desire my husband and I have to see our children fluent in New Testament Greek. My own children have enjoyed learning Greek, and I hope you enjoy it as well. I have tried to make this course simple, but meaty enough to encourage further study. With very few modifications, this can be used as an oral program for younger students or as a written program for those ready to learn how to write in Greek. A motivated student could use this as a self-teaching course, though I think that most students will benefit from having someone to work for/with. The course includes memory work, grammar lessons, review work, and practice exercises. All practice exercises are also included in the student workbook, and an audio CD aids in pronunciation.

Each lesson is broken down into five parts, to correspond to five days of study. At this rate, all thirty lessons can be covered in a standard school year. A younger student may find a slower pace helpful, and the program can easily be extended to cover 1 ½-2 years. My own students have been able to complete each day's work in less than 30 minutes, but you may find yourself working faster or slower depending on your needs.

Begin each day by looking at the four letters you will learn that day. Study the first letter, noticing whether it is similar to any English letters. As you look at it, say its Greek name and the sound it makes. Continue in this way through all four letters. Then cover the names and see if you can name each letter correctly. Once you can name the day's letters, spend some time writing them. Finally, you may find some activities in Appendix F that will help you continue to review until you know all 24 letters.

Most days, there is also some kind of exercise or activity to do, after the review material and any grammar lesson. These assignments can be written out in the workbook or completed orally, whichever you prefer. The student who is capable of doing at least some of his own writing will find that it is worth the effort in the long run, but oral exercises are a great way to introduce the Greek language in a less intense way. The approach you take will depend largely on the age and ability of your student, and your own goals in studying the language. Remember that it is fine to modify this course to fit your needs. The exercises vary in difficulty, and some students may need more help with the difficult assignments, or you may opt to skip them at this point. A student who only memorizes the vocabulary and grammar paradigms will still find that he has a significant advantage if he continues on with Greek. Such a student may wish to return to this course, studying the grammar and completing the translation exercises the second time through.

If your student shows a greater interest in one or more of the elements introduced in this text, encourage them in this interest. Your student may like the word studies and derivative work included in Monday's lesson. There are many more derivatives than the ones I have listed. Such a student would enjoy searching these words out and noticing Greek elements in our own language. Some students may love the idea of learning Biblical texts in the original language. An interlinear New Testament would provide countless verses to study and learn. (In the text, I quote *The NKJV Greek-English Interlinear New Testament*, and there are many other options readily available. Choose one that includes your preferred English translation). Perhaps composing original sentences would appeal to some. Original composition is one of the best ways to become proficient in a foreign language. Again, encourage the interests of your students. Help them to see the value in learning the Greek language.

I hope you enjoy using this text as much as I have enjoyed writing it!

Αὐτῷ ἡ δόξα καὶ νῦν καὶ εἰς ἡμέραν αἰῶνος. ᾿Αμήν.
(To Him be the glory both now and forever. Amen. 2 Peter 3:18)

---

* Arthur L. Farstad et al, eds., *The NKJV Greek-English Interlinear New Testament* (Nashville: Thomas Nelson, 1994).

1

Alphabet & Sounds, PART 1

OBJECTIVE: Begin learning the letters of the
Greek alphabet, so they are recognizable by sound and name.

α Just as you had to learn the letters and sounds of the English alphabet before you could begin reading, you will now have to do the same in Greek. The good news is that the Greek alphabet is even easier to learn than our English alphabet! Many of its 24 letters are very similar (in look and/or sound) to our English letters. If you learn four letters a day, you will have the entire alphabet memorized in only six days.

Begin each day by looking at the four letters you will learn that day. Study the first letter, noticing whether it is similar to any English letters. As you look at it, say its Greek name and the sound it makes. Continue in this way through all four letters. Then cover the names and see if you can name each letter correctly. Once you can name the day's letters, spend some time writing them. Finally, since you will want to keep reviewing the letters until you know all 24, you may find some game or activity suggestions in the appendix section devoted to review that appeal to you.

day 1 : *alpha* through *delta*

α	Alpha	/ă/ as in father
β	Beta	/b/
γ	Gamma	/g/ as in get*
δ	Delta	/d/

* *two gammas together say 'ng'*

You will notice that all four of your letters today have similarities to English letters. Do you see how alpha, beta, and delta look and sound very similar to our English A, B, and D? Gamma, though it does not look much like the letter G, makes the same sound. Notice, though, that the letter gamma always makes the 'hard' /g/ sound, never the 'soft' /g/ sound (It never makes the /j/ sound that begins our word 'giraffe'). Now practice writing the letters you have just learned. As you write each letter, say its name and the sound it makes.

day 2: *epsilon* through *theta*

ε	Epsilon	/ĕ/ as in elephant
ζ	Zeta	/dz/
η	Eta	/ā/ as in ate
θ	Theta	/th/ as in thing

Although epsilon looks enough like an English E that you probably will never forget its sound, you may find the next three letters more unusual. Remember to study these four letters until you can name them and say their sounds, then go back and see how well you remember the letters you learned yesterday. Can you still name them, write them, and tell what sound they make?

Once again, practice writing and saying the letters.

day 3: *iota* through *mu*

ι	Iota	/ĭ/ as in sit or /ē/*
κ	Kappa	/k/
λ	Lambda	/l/
μ	Mu	/m/

*iota does not make the English long i sound. Its name is pronounced 'ee-ota'.

Here again, you can see that our letters I, K, L, and M are similar in sound and form to these Greek letters.

Practice writing and saying the letters, and don't forget to review the letters from previous days.

day 4: *nu* through *pi*

ν	Nu	/n/
ξ	Xi	/x/
o	Omicron	/ō/ as in obey
π	Pi	/p/*

If you have ever come across the symbol π in your math lessons, you are probably accustomed to pronouncing it with the English long 'i' sound at the end ('pie'). It should actually be pronounced with a long 'e' sound ('pea').

The letter nu looks a lot like an English V, though it sounds like an N. Pay special attention to this letter and to the letter xi, as their forms are probably unusual to you.

day 5: Review.

Spend some time today reviewing the alphabet through the letter pi. Try reciting the letter names, and then try doing it with your eyes closed! Match the following Greek letters with the correct name.

Here are some words to try reading:

δόξα   λόγον

λάμβδα   γάμμα

κακόν†

---

†You will notice that Greek words have many little marks above them. These marks are either accent marks or breathing marks. Your students will learn more about breathing marks in lesson 2, so for now we only need to talk about accents. In Greek, there are three accents. They always go over a vowel, and they are the acute ´, the grave `, and the circumflex ˆ. There are three accents, but they all share the same job, which is to show which syllable is stressed. Pay attention to the accents when pronouncing a word, because they will help you to keep your pronunciation consistent. However, it is not necessary to require that a student who is doing his own writing duplicate the accent in his exercises. There are many rules which govern when each accent is used, and they tend to get complicated.

2

Alphabet & Sounds, PART II

OBJECTIVE: Finish learning the letters of the Greek alphabet, so they are recognizable by sound and name.

As you continue learning the Greek alphabet this week, be sure to review the letters you learned last week. You don't want to forget what you have already learned!

day 1:

ρ	Rho	/r/
σ,ς	Sigma	/s/*
τ	Tau	/t/
υ	Upsilon	French /ü/ (similar to the English /ōō/ sound, as in zoo)

*The first form of sigma is used at the beginning or middle of a word, while the second is used at the end.

Although it looks almost exactly like the English P, the letter rho never makes a /p/ sound. The rest of your letters today look very much like their English equivalents, so they should be easy for you to remember.

Practice writing and saying these letters.

day 2:

φ	Phi*	/f/
χ	Chi*	German hard /ch/ as in ach (guttural)
ψ	Psi*	/ps/
ω	Omega	/ō/ as in note

*Remember, the iota is pronounced as a long 'e': Phi= 'fee', Chi= 'chee', Psi= 'psee'.
The Greek alphabet finishes with these four letters. You will probably find them to be the most unusual of all the letters you have learned so far. The Latin language

transliterated the Greek letter φ as *ph*, and we still see this today in some of our words, like *telephone* and *elephant*. The letter ψ shows up in words like *psychology*, and the letter χ in words like *Christian* and *charisma*.

Write and say these letters.

You now know all 24 letters of the alphabet. Can you recite the letters from alpha to omega? Can you remember the sounds well enough to read these Greek words?

Read:

χάρις

καρδία

τέκνον

λαμβάνω

πατρός

day 3: The breathing mark.

Every word beginning with a vowel or diphthong has a breathing mark. The mark goes over the initial vowel or over the second vowel in a diphthong. A rough breathing mark (῾) indicates a 'h' sound at the beginning of the word, while a smooth breathing mark (᾿) indicates that there is no 'h' sound. So, ἑν is pronounced 'hen' and ἐν is pronounced 'en'.

Read:

ἁμαρτία   ὁδός

ἀδελφός   ἔρημος

ἐγώ   ὄχλος

day 4 : Diphthongs.

Diphthongs: these are pretty similar to the corresponding English diphthongs, but here is a chart for easy reference:

αι   sounds like 'ai' in aisle

ει   sounds like 'a' in fate

οι   sounds like 'oi' in oil

αυ   sounds like 'ow' in cow

ευ   sounds like 'eu' in feud

ου   sounds like 'oo' in food

υι   sounds like 'uee' in queen

Read:

δοῦλος

καί

υἱός

ἀλήθεια

αὐτοί

Notes:

Our word 'alphabet' comes from the Greek. Can you see the first two letters of the Greek alphabet in this word? Alpha + Beta = alphabet

The word **omicron** means 'little o' (Think of *micro* as in *micro*scope.) The word **omega** means 'big o.' (Think of a *mega*phone and *mega*lith.)

Revelation 1:8 says, "'I am the Alpha and the Omega, the Beginning and the End,' says the Lord." Notice that Alpha and Omega are at the beginning and end of the Greek alphabet.

day 5: Review.

Review alphabet, diphthongs, and breathing marks. See Appendix F in the back of the book with ideas to help you review.

3

Verbs, PART I

OBJECTIVE: Introduce the present active
indicative conjugation. Begin learning vocabulary.

Memory Verse:

Ἐν ἀρχῇ ἦν ὁ Λόγος

In (the) beginning was the Word

John 1:1a

Each day begin by reading the Memory verse. It may be a little tricky at first to remember the sounds of all the new letters, but it does get easy with practice! After a few days, start seeing how far you can get in the verse without looking at the paper. You will be working on this verse for several weeks, so you will have plenty of time to get used to reading it, and hopefully to memorize it. Each week, we will be adding a new phrase to the verse, until you have successfully memorized all of John 1:1.

Notice that there are a few capital letters in this verse. Although this verse begins with a capital letter, capitals (called *uncials* in Greek) were originally not used to begin sentences. In fact, when the New Testament was first written, spaces were not used between the words either. I, for one, am glad the spaces have been inserted. ἐναρχῆῆνὁλόγος and so on would give me a headache! The uncial forms in this verse are listed here. Pay special attention to these forms and try to remember them as you are introduced to them.

Epsilon: Ε/ε   Lambda: Λ/λ

day 1: Introduction to verbs.

A verb is a word that shows *action*. Walking is an action. In English, we use nouns (the name of a person, place, thing or idea) to show who or what is performing the action. "Mary walks." Sometimes we use pronouns in the place of nouns. Instead of saying "Mary walks", I could use the pronoun 'she'. "She walks." In English, I cannot just say "walk" and expect you to understand what I mean. You do not know if I mean "I walk" or "They walk" or "You walk". We need a pronoun to indicate who is doing the action by telling us the *number* (singular or plural) and the *person* (first, second or third). When you read "she", you knew that there was only one person walking, and that that person was not you yourself (the "first person") or the person with whom you were speaking ("second person"), but someone outside of the conversation (the "third person").

In Greek, however, these pronouns are not needed. This is because the pronoun is included in the verb endings. The English 'we destroy' is translated into a single word λύομεν. 'I destroy' in Greek is λύω. The ending is different, because the pronoun is contained in the ending.

Today you will practice writing in Greek. Carefully copy this week's memory verse in your workbook.

day 2: Vocabulary.

All of the vocabulary words for this week are verbs. Look carefully at these words to see what they all have in common. Practice reading them several times.

> ἀκούω
>
> βλέπω
>
> ἔχω
>
> λύω
>
> πιστεύω

Notice that they all end with an omega.

Here are the English translations:

ἀκούω	I hear
βλέπω	I see
ἔχω	I have or hold

λύω	I loose or destroy
πιστεύω	I believe

Notice that all the translations have the pronoun 'I' in them. The omega stands for the pronoun 'I'. If we change the omega to something else, we are changing the pronoun.

day 3: Present tense verb endings.

Present tense verbs show actions which are happening right now. (As in, "I jump.") If the tense of the verb changes, the endings on the verb will change. (For example, you will be unable to say "I jumped." until you learn the past tense endings.) Below are the verb endings for **present tense verbs.** Each of these endings stands for a pronoun. Recite these several times, and next week we will continue learning how to apply them. To recite them, read down the left column, and then down the right column.

−ω	−ομεν
−εις	−ετε (both epsilons should make a short /ĕ/ sound)
−ει	−ουσι

day 4: Review.

Practice reciting your memory verse and the Greek alphabet. Write the English translations for this week's vocabulary words in your workbook.

day 5: Review.

Don't forget to go over the alphabet again this week. You should be able to recite and write it from start to finish…from alpha to omega. Also, you should be able to read through the Memory verse with some fluency, and be sure you have memorized your vocabulary words.

4

Verbs, PART II

OBJECTIVE: Continue learning the present
active indicative conjugation. Apply to various roots.

Memory Verse:

Ἐν ἀρχῇ ἦν ὁ Λόγος,
in (the) beginning was the Word,

καὶ ὁ Λόγος ἦν πρὸς τὸν Θεόν
and the Word was with the God

John 1:1a,b

This week, you will be working on memorizing the second clause of John 1:1. Continue to review the part you have already memorized, adding this week's phrase onto the phrase from last week.

This week you learn a new uncial form. Theta: Θ/θ

Look back over John 1:1. Notice that several of the words begin with vowels. Are you remembering to pay attention to the breathing mark on those words? Remember that a breathing mark which looks like the letter 'c' indicates that we must make an 'h' sound at the beginning of the word. Looking carefully, you will see that there is only one word (occurring 2 times) which has that breathing mark. It is the word ὁ. Make sure you say "ho" when you read or say this word.

day 1 : Vocabulary.

Here are the vocabulary words for this week. Read over them until you are comfortable pronouncing them.

γινώσκω	I know
γράφω	I write
λαμβάνω	I take
λέγω	I say or speak
πάσχω	I suffer

Today you will practice writing the new portion of your memory verse neatly.

$$\text{καὶ ὁ Λόγος ἦν πρὸς τὸν Θεόν}$$

day 2: Pronouns and verb endings.

Last week we saw that Greek verbs include pronouns. Can you list some subject pronouns in English? Remember that some pronouns cannot be used as the subject of a sentence—we would never say '**Me** went to the store.' or '**Us** jumped.' Try to list only the pronouns that can be used as the subject of a sentence here.

Were you able to list all of these pronouns?

I	We
You	You (plural)
He, she, it	They

Notice that the pronouns as listed above are categorized. All of the singular pronouns (referring to one person) are on the left side, and all of the plural pronouns (referring to more than one person) are on the right side. They are also categorized by person. 'I' and 'we' are together in the top line, since they both refer to the speaker, the "first person." 'You' is the person to whom the speaker speaks, the "second person." And in the bottom line, 'he', 'she', 'it', and 'they' are all outside of the immediate conversation. We call them the "third person."

Here are our Greek verb endings:

−ω	−ομεν
−εις	−ετε
−ει	−ουσι

If ω stands for the pronoun 'I', how do you think you would translate the other endings?

Here is a complete chart with the Greek endings which are equivalent to each of our English subject pronouns.

singular		*plural*	
I	−ω	We	−ομεν
You	−εις	You(p)	−ετε
He	−ει	They	−ουσι

There is one more thing you must know about the ending that stands for the pronoun *they*. If a verb ending in −ουσι (*they*) comes at the end of a sentence, it usually has a nu added to it (-ουσιν). This also happens when the verb is not at the end of the sentence, but it comes before a word that begins with a vowel. So a word like γράφουσι (they write) would become γράφουσιν. This rule is very similar to our rule in English regarding the article *a/an*. This nu, which is sometimes there and sometimes not, is called the *movable nu*.

day 3: Conjugation of verbs.

Now that we know the verb endings, we can conjugate any of the verbs we have learned so far. Conjugate means to write out the different forms of a verb. To conjugate a verb, you must remove the −ω ending from the vocabulary list forms to find the *stem* and then add each of the other endings to the stem.

For example, here is the verb ἀκούω, with an English translation.

ἀκούω	*I hear*	ἀκούομεν	*we hear*
ἀκούεις	*you hear*	ἀκούετε	*you hear*
ἀκούει	*he, she, it hears*	ἀκούουσι	*they hear*

day 4: Practice conjugation.

Conjugate and translate the verbs ἀκούω, ἔχω, λύω, πιστεύω* in your workbook.

day 5: Review.

Review your vocabulary and practice saying your verb endings and memory verse.

---

*This looks like a lot of work, but it may be done orally, and should only take a few minutes. It would be helpful for the students to have a copy of the personal endings in front of them (–ω, –εις, –ει, etc), and then they can quickly add them to the stem.

5

Verbs, PART III

OBJECTIVE: Learn the definition of stems.
Continue practice with conjugation.

Memory Verse:

Ἐν ἀρχῇ ἦν ὁ Λόγος,
in *(the)* *beginning* *was* *the* *Word,*

καὶ ὁ Λόγος ἦν πρὸς τὸν Θεόν,
and *the* *Word* *was* *with* *the* *God*

καὶ Θεὸς ἦν ὁ Λόγος.
and *God* *was* *the* *Word.*

John 1:1

You may notice that the part of John 1:1 which you are memorizing this week is worded slightly differently than it is in your own Bible. In your own Bible, it likely says, "…and the **word** was **God**." Above, the Greek text is translated word for word, and the Greek language has more variety in its sentence structure than we do in English. In Greek, the subject of the sentence is identified by its ending rather than by its place in the sentence (as it is in English). You will learn more about this in the next few weeks.[*]

You should be aiming to have John 1:1 completely memorized by the end of this week (And you should be able to tell what it means in English, too!). Next week, we will begin learning a new verse.

day 1 : Vocabulary.

ὁ ἄγγελος	the messenger, angel
ὁ λόγος	the word
βάλλω	I throw

---

[*]Now, if you have noticed that both θεός and λόγος have the same ending, you may be wondering how translators know that *word* is actually the subject, and not *God*. This is a grammatical point which goes beyond the scope of this text, but when this type of sentence occurs, with a linking verb joining two nouns, if only one of the nouns carries an article, **that** noun is the subject.

διδάσκω	I teach
δέκα	ten

Notice that the word ἄγγελος has a double gamma. Did you remember that this makes a /ng/ sound?

Many of our English words come from Greek words. For example, do you know the English word that means 'ten years'? It is 'decade', isn't it? Look carefully at the vocabulary words above. Do you see which word we borrowed to make our word *decade*? Of course you see that it is δέκα, which means *ten*. A word that is borrowed from a word in another language is called a **derivative**. Can you think of some other derivatives for the words above?

Remember to write neatly as you copy this week's memory work.

καὶ θεὸς ἦν ὁ λόγος.

day 2: Recite verb endings.

When you remove the ending from a verb, the part you are left with is called a *stem*. Removing the ending ω from the word διδάσκω leaves us with the *stem* διδασκ-.

Conjugate διδάσκω and βάλλω in your workbook.

day 3: Practice translating from Greek to English.

When you translate verbs from Greek into English, first identify the personal ending. It will tell you what pronoun to use. Then translate the complete verb phrase.

For βλέπεις we find the ending −εις, which means "you" (singular). We know that the stem means "see". Together we translate, "You (s) see."

It may be helpful to circle or underline the ending (personal pronoun) of the above verbs before translating them.

day 4: Practice translating from English to Greek.

Today you will translate into Greek, but don't get discouraged if you find this more difficult than yesterday's exercise. Translating from English into Greek is harder to do!

"we see"

Find the stem: "see" is βλεπ–
Add the ending: the pronoun "we" is translated as the ending ομεν

βλεπομεν

Now give it a try in your workbook!

day 5: Review vocabulary and alphabet.

6

Irregular Verb εἰμί

OBJECTIVE: Learn the present active indicative
conjugation of εἰμί, the Greek verb "I am."

Ἐγώ εἰμι ἡ ὁδὸς
I   am   the   way
John 14:6a

You should have John 1:1 down well now, so as you continue to review it once a week (more often if you don't have it completely memorized), start working on this verse daily.

day 1 : Vocabulary.

ὁ νόμος	the law
ὁ βίος	the life
ὁ θεός	the God
ὁ ἀγρός	the field
ὁ ἀπόστολος	the apostle

Can you think of some English **derivatives** of these Greek words? Our word *biology* comes from the Greek words βίος and λόγος. You have learned that λόγος means word, but it also can mean *the science or study of something*. Biology, of course, is the study of life.

Can you think of another English derivative which uses one of this week's vocabulary words along with λόγος to mean *the science or study of something*?

Remember to write neatly as you copy this week's memory work.

ἐγώ εἰμι ἡ ὁδὸς

day 2: The irregular verb 'to be'.

Remember that a verb is a word that shows action. *Jump, shout, read, dig,* and *wrestle* are all verbs. A verb can also show **state of being**. *Am, is, are, was,* and *were* are all **being** verbs. This week, we will be learning the present tense conjugation for the 'to be' verb. It is an irregular verb. Not all verbs follow the regular ω, εις, ει endings. When a verb 'breaks the rules' like this, it is called an **irregular verb**. Here is the conjugation for 'to be'.

singular		*plural*
εἰμί	1st person	ἐσμέν
εἶ	2nd person	ἐστέ
ἐστί	3rd person	εἰσὶν

εἰμί means 'I am.' Can you figure out what the rest of the words in the above table mean? Notice that εἰμί is one of the words in your new Memory verse.

For this verb, both the third person singular and the third person plural have a movable nu. Remember that this nu is only added when the word ends a sentence or comes before another word beginning with a vowel. If I wanted to say 'he is an apostle' I would say: ἐστὶν ἀπόστολος. Can you find the movable nu? 'They are apostles' looks like this: εἰσιν ἀπόστολοι. Again, do you see the movable nu?

Although εἰμί is an irregular verb, most verbs in Greek are regular. They use the same endings in the present tense that you have been learning over the past few weeks. Today you will conjugate λύω in your workbook. Remember that it is a regular verb and will use the regular endings you have been learning.

day 3: Practice translating from Greek to English.

Today you will translate from Greek to English. First circle the personal ending, then translate.

day 4: Practice translating from English to Greek.

When you translate into Greek today, look at the pronoun to determine which ending to add to the correct stem.

day 5: Review vocabulary.

You now have 20 vocabulary words to review. Also, be sure you can still recite the alphabet.

α β γ δ ε ζ η θ ι κ λ μ

ν ξ ο π ρ σ τ υ φ χ ψ ω

7

Nouns

OBJECTIVE: Learn the meaning of noun
declensions and memorize an example

Ἐγώ εἰμι ἡ ὁδὸς
I   am   the   way

καὶ ἡ ἀλήθεια
and the   truth
John 14:6a,b

Continue working on John 14:6. Read it through daily:

Last week you learned about the irregular verb εἰμί. You know now that εἰμί means "I am." You may be wondering why the word ἐγώ (I) is used in this sentence, when εἰμί already includes the word 'I'. ἐγώ is not necessary for the sentence to be correct, but it is used for emphasis. One could say that the verse actually says, "**I**, I am the way…"

day 1 : Vocabulary.

ὁ ἀδελφός	the brother
ὁ ἄνθρωπος	the man
ὁ δοῦλος	the slave
ὁ κόσμος	the world
καί	and

The English words *cosmos, cosmopolitan, cosmography, cosmic,* and *cosmology* all are derived from the Greek word κόσμος. Do you know what any of these words mean? Can you use any of them in a sentence? Can you think of any other derivatives for this week's vocabulary words?

Practice writing "and the truth" in Greek on the lines below.

καὶ ἡ ἀλήθεια

day 2: Noun forms in English and Greek.

In English, we don't see a lot of changes in noun forms. If I want to talk about a child, I can say pretty much anything I want about this child without the word changing:*

> The *child* walks.
> Give the *child* the toy.
> He thanked the *child*.

In each of these sentences, the word 'child' has a different job, and yet it looks just the same. If I wanted to talk about something belonging to the child, or something which was the **child**'s, I would have to change my form by adding an **'s**. If I wanted to speak about more than one child, I would have to change my form to **child***ren*. However, for the most part, the word child, and other nouns in the English language, will stay the same regardless of how they are used in the sentence. This is not true in Greek. In Greek, the form of the word tells us what its job is. The words ἀνθρώπου and ἀνθρώπῳ both mean man, but they have different jobs in a sentence, and so they have different forms. Here is a chart of the different forms of the word ἄνθρωπος:

singular	*plural*
ἄνθρωπος	ἄνθρωποι
ἀνθρώπου	ἀνθρώπων
ἀνθρώπῳ	ἀνθρώποις
ἄνθρωπον	ἀνθρώπους

---

* Classifying or diagramming the English sentences which are given as examples (Give that to the child., etc.) may help your student understand how the noun's job differs in each sentence. (There are examples of both classification and diagramming in Appendix E). The word *child* is a subject-noun, an indirect object, and a direct object respectively in each of these sentences above.

Notice that nouns have singular forms and plural forms, just like verbs do. Read through the chart a few times to become familiar with it. To read through it, read down the entire left column first, and then down the right column. Do you see the tiny little mark underneath the omega in the word ἀνθρώπῳ? This little mark is called an **iota subscript**. It does not change the sound of the omega at all. If you look carefully, you will also see iota subscripts appearing from time to time under the η and the α.

You have already learned how the form of a verb changes depending on how it is used. So, both nouns and verbs change their forms in Greek. Remember that when we write a verb out with its different endings, we call that conjugating. Conjugate the verb ἔχω in your workbook.

day 3: Definition of declensions.

The chart above shows us the endings for the word 'man.' These are called **case endings** and they are added on to the **stem**, which in this case is ανθρωπ−.

Identify the case endings in the chart above. You will complete a chart like this in your workbook today.

When I write out a noun in all its parts like this, it is called **declining** the noun. There are groups of nouns which follow the same pattern of endings when they are declined, and each group of nouns is called a **declension**. There are three declensions in Greek, and this is the second declension. It is the easiest declension to learn, so we are learning it first.[*] Whenever you see a noun in your vocabulary words which ends in ος, this is a second declension noun. Look at your vocabulary words for this week. Notice that all of the nouns end in −ος. That means they can all be declined in the same way that ἄνθρωπος was declined above.

day 4: Declensions, continued.

Declensions are always written the same way. The left column is singular, and the

---

[*] The second declension has fewer forms that the first declension. In the second declension, there is a masculine form (which we are learning this week) and a neuter form (which we will learn in Lesson 11). There are also a few feminine nouns which are part of the second declension, but they use the same endings that the masculine nouns use. In contrast, the first declension has three sets of endings for feminine nouns and two sets of endings for masculine nouns.

right column is plural. In our above example, the left side translates as 'man' and the right side translates as 'men.' Each horizontal line is called a case. Later we will learn the names of all the cases, and how some of them are used in sentences. For now, we just need to work on learning the case endings. If we memorize the declension for ἄνθρωπος, we will know the endings for all our second declension nouns ending in ος. And so we are going to recite this chart every day until we know it very well. (Then we will continue reciting it once a week so we don't forget it!) Refer to the chart if you have to, but the sooner you can do it without the chart, the better. Read it through a few times now and see how you do.

day 5 : Review vocabulary and the alphabet.

8

Nouns—Second Declension

OBJECTIVE: Learn the second declension noun endings.

Memory Verse:

Ἐγώ εἰμι ἡ ὁδὸς
I   am   the   way

καὶ ἡ ἀλήθεια
and   the   truth

καὶ ἡ ζωή·
and   the   life;

John 14:6

This week you will be finishing up with John 14:6. Notice that at the end of the verse, there is a semi-colon in the English translation. If you look at the end of the verse in the Greek translation, you may think that there is an error. It looks like only the top half of the semi-colon printed. However, this is the way a semi-colon looks in Greek. The Greek period and comma look just like our period and comma, but if I ask you a question in Greek, it will end with a mark that looks like this: ; That's right—the Greek semi-colon looks like a dot floating in mid-air, and the question mark looks like an English semi-colon.

Now that we have several things we are trying to keep fresh in our memories, I will be reminding you to review something at the beginning of each lesson.

day 1 : Vocabulary.

Every Monday, take the time to review all of your past Memory verses. In the back of the book, all the verses for the year are listed in Appendix C. It is fine to use this for reference, but remember that the goal is to have these verses memorized. Today, try to recite John 1:1, including the English translation.

ὁ θάνατος   the death

ὁ οἶκος   the house

ὁ υἱός   the son

| ὁ κύριος | the lord |
| ὁ λίθος | the stone |

Notice that all the vocabulary words for this week are nouns. What declension are they all part of? An American poet named William Cullen Bryant once wrote a poem called "Thanatopsis." Do your vocabulary words this week give you a clue as to what this poem could be about?

Today you will practice writing the new portion of your memory verse.

καὶ ἡ ζωή·

day 2: Practice declining nouns.

Recite the personal endings for verbs.

Last week we learned that Greek nouns have different endings depending on how they are used in a sentence. To write a noun with all its different endings is called **declining** the noun. To decline the noun, you must first be able to find the stem of the word. (The stem is the part that stays the same.) The endings are added onto the stem. So far, all the nouns we have learned end in ος. To find the stem, we simply remove the ος from the word. Since these nouns all follow the same pattern, we say that they are part of the same **declension**.

Here are the second declension endings that you circled last week:

−ος	−οι
−ου	−ων
−ῳ	−οις
−ον	−ους

Using these endings, let's try to decline the noun θάνατος. First, we remove the ος to show that the stem is θάνατ−. We need to add the endings above to this stem. Now we are ready to decline the noun!

θάνατος	θάνατοι
θανάτου	θανάτων
θανάτῳ	θανάτοις
θάνατον	θανάτους

day 3: Practice declining nouns.

Recite declension of ἄνθρωπος.

singular	*plural*
ἄνθρωπ____	ἄνθρωπ____
ἀνθρώπ____	ἀνθρώπ____
ἀνθρώπ____	ἀνθρώπ____
ἄνθρωπ____	ἀνθρώπ____

day 4: Verb review.

Recite conjugation for εἰμί (I am).

singular		*plural*
εἰμί	1st person	ἐσμέν
εἶ	2nd person	ἐστέ
ἐστί	3rd person	εἰσί

Have you remembered to practice your memory verse each day? See if you can recite it from memory.

day 5: Review.

Review all of the vocabulary you have learned until now. Use your flashcards and quiz yourself.

9

Sentences, PART I

OBJECTIVE: Begin translating simple
sentences in the subject-verb pattern.

Memory Verse:

Νυνὶ δὲ μένει πίστις, ἐλπίς, ἀγάπη,
Now and remains faith, hope, love,

I Corinthians 13:13a

Do you know John 14:6 well enough to begin a new memory verse? Our next verse is probably confusing you right now. You may be thinking that it doesn't make any sense. Remember that Greek sentence structure sometimes differs from English sentence structure. In English, all of I Corinthians 13:13 would be translated, *"And now remain (or abide) faith, hope, love, these three; but the greatest of these is love."* Over the next few weeks, we will be memorizing all of this verse.

Notice that the uncial form of nu (ν) is **N**.

day 1 : Vocabulary.

ὁ οὐρανός	the heaven
ὁ τόπος	the place
ἐγείρω	I raise up
ἄγω	I lead
μένω	I remain

Notice that some of your vocabulary words this week are nouns and some are verbs. You can tell which are nouns and which are verbs without even knowing what they mean in English. All of the nouns end in ος and all the verbs end in the personal pronoun ω, which means 'I'.

Topography, topology, and *toponym* are all English derivatives of the Greek word τόπος. Topography is the description of a place, topology is the study of a place, and toponym is the name of a place.

Carefully write this week's verse.

Νυνὶ δὲ μένει πίστις, ἐλπίς, ἀγάπη,

day 2 : Learn about nominative case.

Review personal endings for verbs.

This week we are going to begin writing sentences in Greek. Remember that a sentence must express a complete thought. This means that usually a sentence has **at least** a subject-noun and a verb. In Greek, we show that a noun is the subject of the sentence by putting it in the **Nominative Case**. The Nominative case is on the first line of the declension.

singular		*plural*
ἄνθρωπος	Nominative	ἄνθρωποι
ἀνθρώπου	Genitive	ἀνθρώπων
ἀνθρώπῳ	Dative	ἀνθρώποις
ἄνθρωπον	Accusative	ἀνθρώπους

Here you can see the names of all the cases. Right now don't worry too much about them. Just try to remember that the nominative case shows the subject of the sentence, and that the nominative is always the first line of the declension.

One of your vocabulary words is μένω. Can you find a conjugated form of μένω in this week's memory verse?

day 3 : First sentences .

Recite declension of ἄνθρωπος. You should be able to do this without looking it up. If this is still difficult, remember to practice every day.

So, we know that sentences need a subject and a verb, and we know to use the nominative case for the subject in Greek. We know how to say "I see" (βλέπω) or "you see" (βλέπεις), but what if I wanted to say "An apostle sees."? First we need to know that in Greek, there is no word for 'a' or 'an'. Then, we need to find the word for 'apostle', and we need to make sure it is in the nominative case. Since we are talking about one apostle, we need to make sure we will use the singular nominative ending and not the plural. The word we need is ἀπόστολος. (ος is the singular nominative ending.) Next, we need the correct form of the word 'sees.' Since in our sentence 'apostle' could be replaced with the pronoun 'he', we need to use βλέπει (he sees). So, here is our first Greek sentence: ἀπόστολος βλέπει. Remember, in Greek, we don't even have to start the sentence with a capital letter.

Before you translate a sentence into Greek, classify it so that you know what each word's job is. Ask "Who or what is this sentence about?" and mark that word *S* for *subject*. Then ask, "What did subject do?" The answer to that question is marked *V* for *verb*. When you translate a sentence, the subjects will have a nominative case ending and the verbs will have a personal ending.*

>   *A brother writes.*
>   Who or what is this sentence about? A brother.
>   This is the subject of your sentence.
>
>   What case do we use for the subject of the sentence?
>   Is the subject singular or plural?
>   ἀδελφός is the nominative, singular form of the word *brother*.
>
>   What does the brother do? This is the verb in your sentence.
>   Does this sentence refer to the 1st person (I or we), the 2nd person (you), or the 3rd person (he, she, it or they)? Will we use the singular or plural ending?
>   γράφει is the 3rd person, singular form of *write*.

ἀδελφός γράφει.

Congratulations! You are now ready to translate your first sentences into Greek. Continue

---

* Students may think it is silly to classify such simple sentences. *Of course* they know what the subject of the sentence is! But it is a good habit to get into now, while the sentences are easy. When the sentences get more complicated, it is a great help to know and mark what each word's function is in the sentence, to be assured that you are using the right case.

to ask yourself these questions as you translate sentences in your workbook.

day 4: Translate sentences with plural subjects.

Recite the conjugation for irregular verb εἰμί.

If you look at the chart for ἄνθρωπος again, you probably can find the nominative plural form of that word. It is ἄνθπωποι. οι is the nominative plural ending for second declension nouns. Because we know this, we know how to have plural subjects in our sentences. "Apostles see" is not too hard to translate into Greek. First, the word for 'apostles' is ἀπόστολοι. The word for 'see' must be βλέπουσι, because ουσι is the personal ending that means 'they'. Finally, to translate this sentence correctly, we must remember the *movable nu*. So, "Apostles (they) see" looks like this: ἀπόστολοι βλέπουσιν.

Yesterday we translated the sentence, "A brother writes." But what if there were two brothers? Or three? We would say, "Brothers write." To translate the sentence into Greek, we would ask the same questions we asked yesterday.

> *Brothers write.*
>> Who or what is this sentence about? Brothers.
>> This is the subject of your sentence.
>>
>> What case do we use for the subject of the sentence?
>> Is the subject singular or plural?
>> ἀδελφόι is the nominative, singular for of the word *brother*.
>>
>> What do the brothers do? This is the verb in your sentence.
>> Does this sentence refer to the 1st person (I or we), the 2nd person (you), or the 3rd person (he, she, it or they)? Will we use the singular or plural ending?
>>
>> γράφουσι is the 3rd person, plural form of *write*.

Since ουσι comes at the end of a sentence, we will add the movable nu.

ἀδελφοὶ γράφουσιν.

day 5: Review vocabulary.

Time for another round of Greek memory, or your own favorite vocabulary review.

10

Sentences, PART II

OBJECTIVE : Continue translating simple sentences.

Memory Verse:

Νυνὶ δὲ μένει πίστις, ἐλπίς, ἀγάπη,
now   and   remains   faith,   hope,   love,

τὰ τρία ταῦτα·
the   three   these;

I Corinthians 13:13a,b

As you memorize I Corinthians 13:13, keep in mind the way the wording of the verse changes in an English translation. *"And now remain (or abide) faith, hope, love, these three; but the greatest of these is love."*

day 1 : Vocabulary.

πέμπω	I send
φέρω	I bear, bring
βαπτίζω	I baptize
κρίνω	I judge
ὁ διδάσκαλος	the teacher

Have you ever heard of someone or something referred to as *didactic?* Didactic refers to an ability to teach. We may say that the teacher's tone was very *didactic*, or instructive.

We may say that games are not always *didactic*. Our word didactic is derived from the same root as the Greek word διδάσκαλος.

Write this week's portion of I Corinthians 13:13:

τὰ τρία ταῦτα·

Review John 1:1 and John 14:6.

day 2 : Nominative case nouns.

Review verb conjugations.

Answer each of the following questions orally. If you are unsure of the answer, look back through the previous lessons to review.

Do you remember which noun case is used as the subject of the sentence?

When you are looking at a declension chart, on which line do you find the nominative case?

In the second declension, what are the endings for the nominative singular and the nominative plural?

day 3 : Translate sentences into Greek.

Review declension of ἄνθρωπος. Say it aloud.

A sentence does not always have a noun as the subject. If we want the subject of our sentence to be a pronoun instead of a noun, then the sentence only needs to have one word in it, because in Greek, the pronouns are included in the verbs as personal endings. So the sentence "He suffers." is translated "πάσχει." English sentences need two words in order to be complete: a subject noun and a verb. In Greek, one word can convey a complete thought.

day 4 : Translate sentences into English.

Review conjugation for irregular verb εἰμί.

Translate this sentence into English.

ἀπόστολοι βλέπουσιν.

First find the verb. Look for the $-\omega$, $-\varepsilon\iota\varsigma$, $-\varepsilon\iota$, $-o\mu\varepsilon\nu$, $-\varepsilon\tau\varepsilon$, or $-ou\sigma\iota$ ending.
Is this verb singular or plural? How do you know?
Does the ending indicate a first, second, or third person pronoun?

The word βλέπουσιν has a third person plural ending. The ending tells me that "they" are performing the action. The stem, βλέπ–, tells me the action: see. We translate βλέπουσιν as "they see."

If there were no other words in your sentence, your translation now would be complete. However, there is another word.

Does it have a noun ending or a verb ending?
What case does the ending indicate?
Is it singular or plural?
This ending shows that the word plays which part in this sentence?

The word ἀπόστολοι has a nominative plural ending. The nominative ending tells us that it is the subject of our sentence. And we know that it is plural. The subject of our sentence is "apostles".

Now make sure your sentence is in proper English word order.

Apostles see.

We do not use the word "they" for our subject, because it would be redundant in English.

day 5: Review vocabulary.

As always on Day 5, review the vocabulary you have learned so far this year. Also use this time to practice any memory verses and grammar forms (conjugations and declensions) that you don't know perfectly.

11

Second Declension, Neuter

OBJECTIVE: Become familiar with
the second declension neuter paradigm.

Νυνὶ δὲ μένει πίστις, ἐλπίς, ἀγάπη,
now   and   remains   faith,   hope,   love,

τὰ τρία ταῦτα·
the   three   these;

μείζων δὲ τούτων ἡ ἀγάπη.
(the) greatest   but   of these   the   love (is).

I Corinthians 13:13

As you memorize I Corinthians 13:13, keep in mind the way the wording of the verse changes in an English translation. *"And now remain (or abide) faith, hope, love, these three; but the greatest of these is love."*

day 1 : Vocabulary.

τό τέκνον	the child
τό εὐαγγέλιον	the gospel
τό πρόσωπον	the face
τό ἱερόν	the temple
τό δῶρον	the gift

The word εὐαγγέλιον is made out of two parts. First, the prefix εὐ means good. Looking at the rest of the word, we see that αγγέλιον looks very similar to another word you have already learned—ἄγγελος. You should remember that ἄγγελος means *angel* or *messenger*, and this word, ἀγγέλιον, has a related meaning. ἀγγέλιον means *message*. The entire word together, εὐαγγέλιον, literally means *good message*, or good news. Our words **evangelize** and **evangelist** come directly from this Greek word.

Write this week's portion of I Corinthians 13:13:

μείζων δὲ τούτων ἡ ἀγάπη.

Review John 1:1 and John 14:6.

day 2: Begin learning about the second declension neuter.

Conjugate the verbs ἄγω and γινώσκω in your workbook.

Remember that in Greek there are three noun declensions. That means that there are three groups of endings for nouns. Right now, we are learning about the second declension. We have learned that words ending in −ος are part of the second declension. However, these are not the only words in the second declension. Look at this week's vocabulary words. Notice that they are all nouns—they all name a person, place, or thing. Also notice that they do **not** end in −ος.

In Greek, all nouns are either masculine, feminine, or neuter. This is called their **gender.** It is important for us to learn every noun's gender because the gender of a noun often decides which declension it is in, and it also shows us which form to use for words like adjectives, which must **agree with the noun.** (This means that the adjectives must have the same gender as the noun.) There are two kinds of nouns in the second declension—masculine nouns and neuter nouns. The nouns ending in ος are masculine nouns, and the nouns ending in ον are neuter. This week's vocabulary words are all neuter nouns.

day 3: Introduction to the second declension neuter paradigm.

Review declension of ἄνθρωπος.

The second declension is often called the 'o' declension. This is because the endings in this declension almost always have an omicron or an omega in them.

Here is the declension for δῶρον, which means gift.

singular		*plural*
δῶρον	Nominative	δῶρα
δώρου	Genitive	δώρων
δώρῳ	Dative	δώροις
δῶρον	Accusative	δῶρα

Now go back and look at the endings above. There are several things to notice about these endings. First of all, neuter nouns always have the same endings in the nominative and accusative cases. So when you say this declension, you will always begin and end each side with the same word. That makes it easier, doesn't it? Now, look at the two cases there in the middle, the genitive and the dative. Notice that their endings are just like the masculine endings, which you have already learned. Can you find the only two endings which do not have an omicron or an omega in them? See how the nominative and accusative plural both end with an alpha?

You will be memorizing these endings, and I think you will find them to be pretty easy to remember. Read them through a few times right now, to get used to them.

day 4: Declining second declension neuter nouns.

Review the conjugation for irregular verb εἰμί.

This week we have been learning about second declension neuter nouns. The second declension neuter endings are:

ον	α
ου	ων
ῳ	οις
ον	α

Using these endings, you should be able to decline τέκνον, εὐαγγέλιον, πρόσωπον, and ἱερόν in your notebook. Remember to remove the −ον so you have the stem, and then add the above endings onto that stem.

day 5: Review vocabulary and alphabet.

12

Second Declension, Neuter

OBJECTIVE: Use the second declension neuter, nominative case, in sentences.

Memory Verse:

Νυνὶ δὲ μένει πίστις, ἐλπίς, ἀγάπη,
now   and   remains   faith,   hope,   love,

τὰ τρία ταῦτα·
the   three   these;

μείζων δὲ τούτων ἡ ἀγάπη.
(the) greatest but   of these   the   love (is).

I Corinthians 13:13

This week we are still working on I Corinthians 13:13.

day 1 : Vocabulary.

τό βιβλίον	the book
τό δαιμόνιον	the demon
τό ἔργον	the work
τό πλοῖον	the boat
ὁ ἁμαρτωλός	the sinner

Notice that almost all of your vocabulary words end in –ον. This means that they are part of the second declension and that they are neuter. Second declension neuter nouns end in –ον. The last word on your list, however, is different. Do you remember the declension and gender of words ending in –ος?

Looking over this list of words, you can probably find several which have English derivatives that you are familiar with. Look at the word above for 'book.' The Bible is God's book, isn't it? Doesn't Bible look like βιβλίον? And the word demon is very similar to δαιμόνιον.

Remember that a derivative is a word which we have borrowed from another language (in this case, Greek). If you look up 'erg' in an English dictionary, you will find that this word is used in science to talk about work and energy. It, of course, comes from the Greek word ἔργον.

Review past Memory verses.

day 2: Parsing nouns.

Review verb conjugations. Conjugate the verbs πέμπω and πιστεύω in your workbook.

For a few weeks now, we have been writing sentences using subjects and verbs. All of our sentences so far have had masculine nouns, because until last week, those are all the nouns we knew. Now we are ready to start using neuter nouns in sentences also. These nouns will still be the subjects of our sentences, so they will still be in the **nominative** case. Look at your chart of δῶρον from last week and find the nominative singular and the nominative plural endings.

The nominative singular is −ον, of course, and the nominative plural is −α. These are the endings we will be using in our sentences this week.

Today we are going to *parse* nouns, all in the nominative case. Beside each noun in your workbook, you will write an M or an N, for masculine or neuter (gender). Then write an S or a P, for singular or plural (number). Then translate the word into English. Writing out the parts of a noun like this is called *parsing* the noun.

	gender	number	translation
οὐρανοί	M	P	heavens

day 3: Translating sentences from English to Greek.

Review declension of ἄνθρωπος and δῶρον.

Now we are ready to try some sentences. Before you translate a sentence into Greek, remember to classify it.

A child hears.
>Who or what is this sentence about? This is your subject. Mark it with an S. The subject must always be in the nominative case.
>Is this subject singular or plural?
>Is it masculine or neuter?

τέκνον is the Greek word for child. It is nominative, singular and neuter.

>What does the subject do? This is your verb. Mark it with a V. Verbs must agree with the subject in number and person. Are we referring to a first, second or third person subject?
>Is the subject singular or plural?

ἀκούει is the Greek word for hears. It is 3ʳᵈ person, singular.

τέκνον ἀκούει.

You will translate more sentences in your workbook today. Remember to ask yourself questions as you go.

day 4: Translating sentences from Greek to English.

Review conjugation for irregular verb εἰμί.

Today we will translate sentences into English. For the neuter second declension nouns, remember that the nominative case endings are −ov for the singular and

–α for the plural.

ἱερόν μένει.

Which word is my verb? (Look for verb endings.)
Is it first, second or third person? Is it singular or plural?

μένει is a 3ʳᵈ person singular verb. He, she or it *remains*.

What kind of word is ἱερόν?

ἱερόν is a singular, neuter noun in the nominative case. It must be my subject. It means "temple".

A temple remains.

day 5: Review vocabulary.

13

Using εἰμί in Sentences

OBJECTIVE: Use the linking verb εἰμί in sentences.

Memory Verse:

Πάντοτε χαίρετε
Always   *rejoice*

I Thessalonians 5:16

Are you ready for a new Memory verse? This is from the book of I Thessalonians, and it is a very short verse. In fact, it is so short that you should only need one week to memorize it. Remember to read this verse every day before you begin your lesson.

day 1: Vocabulary.

ὁ ἄρτος	the bread
σώζω	I save
βαίνω	I go
ὁ τυφλός	the blind man
Ἰησοῦς	Jesus

Notice that two of your words this week are common nouns. Do you know the declension they are part of? What gender are they? Two of your words are verbs. Notice that the verbs end in omega, which stands for the personal pronoun 'I'. Your final word, Ἰησοῦς, is a proper noun. It is capitalized (the first letter is the uncial iota), because names are capitalized in Greek just as they are in English. The letters iota and eta, when they are together, do not form a diphthong. Both letters are pronounced, so you will read this "Ee-ay-SOOS."

Write this week's memory verse:

Πάντοτε χαίρετε!

Read over your new verse several times. Also, review past Memory verses. Be sure to say each verse both in Greek and English.

day 2: Review verb conjugations.

Conjugate the verbs σώζω and βαίνω in your workbook.

Several weeks ago, you began memorizing the conjugation for the irregular verb 'to be'. This week, you will be using this verb to write some sentences. The verb 'to be' is called a **linking verb**. Most verbs are called **action verbs** because they show action, such as *jump, roll, sleep,* and *write*. These are all things we do. But 'to be' is a linking verb. It links one side of the sentence (the subject noun) to the other side of the sentence (the predicate nominative).

Here is an example: *The man is an apostle.*

> *Man* is the subject noun of this sentence. It tells whom the sentence is about.

> *Is* is the verb. It links the word man to the word apostle.

> *Apostle* is the predicate nominative in the sentence.

Now, here is a question to think about. Remember that in Greek, nouns have different cases to show what their jobs are in a sentence. We know that the subject of a sentence takes the nominative case. What case do you think the predicate nominative takes? If you said nominative as well, you are correct. Our English name, predicate nominative, gives you a clue, doesn't it? **Nouns that come after a linking verb**, like *apostle* in the sentence above, **take the nominative case**.

Let's look at our sample again.

> S   LV   PN
> The man is an apostle.
> ὁ ἄνθρωπος ἐστιν ἀπόστολος.*

day 3: Review declensions for ἄνθρωπος and δῶρον.

Today we will translate a few sentences. We'll practice here, then continue in your workbook.

A field is a place.

What is this sentence about? That is our subject. Mark it with an S. What case must we use for the subject of a sentence? Is our subject singular or plural?

ἀγρός is the nominative singular form of the word for *field*.

In this sentence, the field does not *do* anything – there is no action – but it does *equal* something. Which word shows this? That word is our linking verb. Mark it with an LV.

To translate this word, you must know whether the subject it refers to is 1ˢᵗ, 2ⁿᵈ or 3ʳᵈ person, and whether it is singular or plural.

ἐστί is the 3ʳᵈ person singular form of the word *to be*.

What does the subject (field) equal? This is the predicate nominative. Mark it with a PN. The predicate nominative must be in the **nominative** case. In this sentence, is it singular or plural?

τόπος is the nominative singular form of the word for *place*.

---

*Perhaps you are familiar with the fact that in Greek, as in other inflected languages, word order is not as important as it is in English. It would be possible to restate my sample sentence (ὁ ἄνθρωπος ἐστι ἀπόστολος.) as ἀπόστολος ἐστι ὁ ἄνθρωπος. If I did this, how would I know whether 'man' or 'apostle' were the subject of my sentence? Notice the small word ὁ. This is the word 'the'. When a linking verb is used in a sentence, the word 'the' is often used to point us to the subject of the sentence. It is like a little flag, saying, "Here is the subject!" Now you can look back at John 1:1. Notice the phrase θεὸς ἦν ὁ λόγος. We translate it "the word was God" even though the exact word order says, "God was the word." The flag word ὁ before the word λόγος tells us that λόγος is the subject of the sentence.

	SN	LV	PN
A	field	is	a place.

ἀγρός ἐστι τόπος.

day 4: Review conjugation for irregular verb εἰμί.

Today you will translate sentences into English in your workbook. Remember that sometimes the personal pronoun (which is part of every verb) is the subject of the sentence. For instance, "He is a slave" in English would be "ἐστί δοῦλος" in Greek.

day 5: Review vocabulary.

14

The Genitive Case

OBJECTIVE: To learn the function of the genitive case.

Memory Verse:

"Ἐγώ εἰμι τὸ Ἄλφα καὶ τὸ Ὦ,"
I   am   the   Alpha   and   the   Omega

Revelation 1:8

This verse contains several uncial letters. (Uncial is the Greek term for a capital letter) The uncial form for epsilon and alpha will remind you of our English counterparts for these letters, and they will be easy for you to spot and to pronounce. However, it is possible that before today you were unfamiliar with the uncial form for omega (Ω/ω), which you see above.

Read this verse every day before you begin your lesson.

day 1: Review past Memory verses.

Vocabulary: This week, instead of learning new vocabulary words, we will review some words you have previously learned. Quiz yourself with these words, seeing how many you can translate into English. Spend extra time this week studying any words you did not remember.

ἀκούω	ὁ βιός
δέκα	ὁ ἄγγελος
πάσχω	ὁ κόσμος
ὁ λίθος	μένω
ὁ οὐρανός	πέμπω

Write this week's memory verse.

"Ἐγώ εἰμι τὸ Ἄλφα καὶ τὸ Ὦ,"

day 2: Conjugate the verbs πέμπω and πιστεύω in your workbook

For a few weeks now, we have been writing sentences with subjects and verbs. Today we are going to learn how to add something else to our sentences. Look at the charts of noun endings below.

Second Declension Masculine Endings

singular		plural
−ος	Nominative	−οι
−ου	Genitive	−ων
−ῳ	Dative	−οις
−ον	Accusative	−ους

Second Declension Neuter Endings

singular		plural
−ον	Nominative	−α
−ου	Genitive	−ων
−ῳ	Dative	−οις
−ον	Accusative	−α

We have learned about the nominative case, which we can use for the subject or predicate nominative of a sentence. If you look right below the nominative case, you will see that the next case is called **the genitive case**. Today we are going to learn about the genitive case.

The genitive case is used in Greek to show **possession.** That means that it shows when something belongs to someone. In English, we use **'s** to show this. We can also use the phrase 'of the…' instead of the **'s**. If I say, "Mary's dog was barking," the word **Mary's** is a possessive. In Greek, it would be in the genitive case. I could also say, "The dog **of Mary** was barking." While this sounds a little funny, sometimes it is easier to think of the possessive in this way when we are translating sentences.

What is the possessive in this sentence?

The fat black hen ate the rooster's grain.

Right, it's "rooster's". What about this one?

The son of the old man was kind.

In this one, it's the whole phrase, 'of the man'.

day 3: Review declension for ἄνθρωπος and δῶρον. Decline the word τόπος orally.

Now that we know that the genitive case shows possession, let's look at the charts above again. What ending do we use for a noun in the singular genitive case? Notice that it is the ending ου. If the word were plural, we would use the ending ων. Now that we know this, we know that ἀνθρώπου means **man's** or **of a man** and we know that ἀνθρώπων means **men's** or **of men**. If you look at the chart for δῶρον, you will see that the masculine and neuter have the same endings in the genitive case. We are getting ready to write sentences such as these: "The man's slave believes." and "The men's sons write."

We have already learned one odd thing about Greek sentences—they do not need to start with a capital letter. Here is another odd thing about Greek sentences—it does not matter what order the words go in. In English, I must say, "The man's slave believes" because if I were to switch the order of the words, it wouldn't make any sense. Nobody would ever say "The slave man's believes." But in Greek, it is very different. Because the nominative case and the genitive case and every other case have their own ending, the words can go in almost any order. The endings will still tell us what the word's job is. When I see a noun in the nominative case, no matter where it is in the sentence, I know that it will be either the subject of the sentence or a predicate nominative. The ending gives it away.

day 4: Recite conjugation for irregular verb εἰμί.

Now we are ready to try a few sentences, using the new information we learned this week. At first it may seem like a lot to remember, but by taking it slow, you'll realize it isn't too hard. I will go through the first one with you. To start, read the sentence and note the endings on each of the words.

εὐαγγέλιον κύριου διδάσκει.

First find the verb. Look at its ending. Is it singular or plural? What personal pronoun does the ending indicate?

διδάσκει is the 3ʳᵈ person singular form of 'to teach'. *He teaches.*

Next find the word that is in the nominative case. Remember, this is your subject. It will either end in –ος /–ον or –οι /–α, depending on whether it is singular or plural, masculine or neuter.

εὐαγγέλιον is the nominative singular form of 'gospel'. It's a neuter noun. *Gospel* is the subject-noun.

Finally, if there is another word in your sentence, and it ends in –ου or – ω ν , this word is in the genitive case, and it is a possessive. Remember to pay attention to whether this word is singular or plural to be sure you translate it accurately.

κύριου is the genitive singular form of the word 'lord'. *of a lord*

εὐαγγέλιον κυρίου διδάσκει.
A gospel of a lord teaches.

Keep these steps in mind as you do your translations in your workbook.

day 5: Review vocabulary.

15

The Genitive Case

OBJECTIVE: Continue learning about the genitive case, including translation of sentences.

Memory Verse:

"Ἐγώ εἰμι τὸ Ἄλφα καὶ τὸ Ὦ,"
I   am   the   Alpha   and   the   Omega

Λέγει Κύριος ὁ Θεός,
Says   Lord   the   God,

Revelation 1:8a,b

Remember to read this verse every day before you begin your lesson. The uncial forms in this week's verse are all ones you have learned previously: Λ/λ, Κ/κ, Θ/θ.

day 1 : Review past Memory verses.

This week, we will review some vocabulary again. Try translating these words into English. Make a note of the ones you do not remember, and spend extra time reviewing them.

ὁ τόπος	ὁ τυφλός
ἐγείρω	τό πλοῖον
πιστεύω	ὁ ἄρτος
ὁ ἄγρος	τό πρόσωπον
λαμβάνω	κρίνω

Copy the new portion of your memory verse in your workbook. Be sure to write carefully.

Λέγει Κύριος ὁ Θεός,

day 2: Conjugate the verbs βαπτίζω and φέρω in your workbook

Last week we learned about the genitive case. Now we know how to use two of the four cases. The nominative case is usually used as a subject of a sentence (though it is also used for predicate nominatives), and the genitive case is used to show possession, like our apostrophe-s in English.

Today we are going to *parse* some Greek words. When we parse a noun, we identify its characteristics. We need to decide the case (nominative or genitive), number (singular or plural) and gender (masculine or neuter) of each word before we translate. When you translate the genitive into English, use the phrase *of a...* rather than an apostrophe-s.

day 3: Review declension for ἄνθρωπος and δῶρον

Today you will translate some words from English into Greek. As you translate, you will need to decide what case ending to use, and whether the word is singular or plural.

day 4: Recite conjugation for irregular verb εἰμί

Ready to translate a few sentences? Before you translate, classify the sentences by marking the subject nouns and verbs.

SN   *V*

A temple of God remains.

What case ending will the subject noun need? Is it singular or plural?

ἱερόν

Remember that the verb must agree with the subject in person and number.

μένει

Then underline every *of...* phrase you can find. Mark these *poss* for possessive, and remember to translate them into the genitive case.

θεου

SN   *poss.*   *V*
A temple <u>of God</u> remains.

Now translate.

ἱερόν μένει θέου.

day 5: Review vocabulary.

If you are playing Memory, you may be ready to take out some of the words you know really well, so the game doesn't take too long to play.

16

First Declension Nouns

"Ἐγώ εἰμι τὸ Ἄλφα καὶ τὸ Ὦ,"
I   am   the   Alpha   and   the   Omega

Λέγει Κύριος ὁ Θεός,
Says   Lord   the   God,

Ὁ ὢν καὶ ὁ ἦν καὶ ὁ ἐρχόμενος,
The one being   and the one who was and the   one coming
Revelation 1:8a,b,c

Remember to read this verse every day before you begin your lesson. The line that you are learning this week is difficult to translate word for word. The word ὁ, which means 'the', is here used as 'the one', but in the New King James version, this portion of the verse is translated "…who is and who was and who is to come."

day 1 : Review past Memory verses.

Vocabulary:

ἡ ἀλήθεια	the truth
ἡ βασιλεία	the kingdom
ἡ ἐκκλησία	the church
ἡ ἡμέρα	the day
ἡ ὥρα	the hour

Notice that all the vocabulary words this week end in alpha. They are all nouns, but they are not part of the second declension, like the other nouns you have learned so far. Nouns that end in **alpha** are part of the **first declension**.

The Greek word ὥρα has an obvious English derivative in our word *hour*. If you are familiar with the English word *ecclesiastical*, then you probably recognize that in the Greek word for church. A more unusual derivative is the word *basil*, which comes from the Greek root βασιλ- (words referring to king, royal, kingdom, etc.),found in this week's word βασιλεία. The herb, *basil*, which is common in cooking, has a name derived from this royal Greek root. Some say that the name refers to basil's strong (kingly) scent, and some say it refers more specifically to sacred qualities attributed to the herb by ancient people.

Write the new portion of your memory verse as neatly as you can in the workbook.

Ὁ ὢν καὶ ὁ ἦν καὶ ὁ ἐρχόμενος,

day 2: Conjugate the verbs ἐγείρω and μένω in your workbook.

Now that we are familiar with second declension nouns, we are going to begin to look at the first declension. Remember, in Greek, there are three declensions in all. This year, we will be learning about two of them. Our goal is to know the first and second declensions very well.

Second declension nouns are usually either masculine or neuter. We can almost always tell the gender of the word by the ending. This is true for first declension nouns also. First declension nouns end in *alpha* or *eta*. First declension nouns are also almost always **feminine**. We can remember that **masculine** nouns end in −ος, **neuter** nouns end in −ον, and **feminine** nouns end in −α or −η. There are a few exceptions to this rule, but we will not be learning many of them this year.

day 3: Review declensions of ἄνθρωπος and δῶρον.

Here is a chart of endings for the first declension noun ἀλήθεια.

ἀλήθεια	nominative	ἀλήθειαι
ἀληθείας	genitive	ἀληθειῶν
ἀληθείᾳ	dative	ἀληθείαις
ἀλήθειαν	accusative	ἀληθείας

Remember that ἀλήθεια means *truth*. So what does ἀλήθειαι mean?
Read through this declension a few times. Remember to read down the left column first and then down the right column. The stem for ἀλήθεια is ἀλήθει-. The first declension endings are added onto this stem. Now go back and find the endings in the chart above. These are the endings you will have to learn. In the coming weeks, you will be reciting the first declension each day until you know it well, and then at least once a week from then on.

day 4: Recite the conjugation for the irregular verb εἰμί.

Today we have some new words which we can use in sentences. If we want to write a sentence in which the subject is a first declension noun, the subject still needs to be in the nominative case, of course. The endings for the first declension nominative are different than the second declension endings, but they are still found on the first line of the chart. Look at your chart and see that the nominative singular ending is −α and the nominative plural ending is −αι.

day 5: Review vocabulary.

17

First Declension Nouns Ending in η

OBJECTIVE : To learn first declension nouns ending in eta, and to use them in sentences.

"Ἐγώ εἰμι τὸ Ἄλφα καὶ τὸ Ὦ,"
I am the Alpha and the Omega

Λέγει Κύριος ὁ Θεός,
Says Lord the God,

"Ὁ ὢν καὶ ὁ ἦν καὶ ὁ ἐρχόμενος,
The one being and the one who was and the one coming

Ὁ Παντοκράτωρ."
The Almighty.

Revelation 1:8

This is your final week learning this verse. You should be able to recite the entire text of Revelation 1:8 by the end of this week.

day 1 : Review Memory verses.

Vocabulary:

ἡ γραφή	the writing, Scripture
ἡ παραβολή	the parable
ἡ εἰρήνη	the peace
ἡ ἐντολή	the commandment
ἡ ζωή	the life

There are many common English derivatives for this week's vocabulary words. Can you think of some of them? Notice that the word γραφή is simply the noun form of a word you learned earlier this year as a verb—γράφω. What about the word εἰρήνη… does this word remind you of any English derivatives? Perhaps you have heard of the name Irene. Irene means peace, and it comes from this Greek word. We also have another word that we use to describe a person with a calm, peaceful nature. The word is *irenic*, and it also comes from εἰρήνη.

Every day this week, read through the paradigm for first declension feminine nouns that you began learning last week. You will need to practice reciting this paradigm frequently if you are going to master it.

Copy the last phrase of Revelation 1:8 as neatly as possible.

Ὁ Παντοκράτωρ.

day 2: Conjugate the verbs ἄγω and γινώσκω in your workbook.

Remember that in Greek there are three declensions for nouns—three groups of endings. We are learning two of them right now. Today we are going to make a list of words in the first declension and a list of words in the second declension. Go through all of your vocabulary flashcards and decide whether or not they are nouns. For every noun, place it under the correct list.

<u>First Declension</u>   <u>Second Declension</u>

I am guessing that this exercise was not too difficult for you. The endings make it pretty easy to tell which words go in which list. All of your words in the first declension end with an −α and all your words in the second declension end with −ος or −ον. But what did you do with this week's vocabulary words? If you look at them, you will see that they are all nouns—they all name a person, place or thing. But they do not end in −α, or −ος, or −ον. These words all end in an −η, and they are part of the first declension as well. Why don't you add them to your first declension list right now?

day 3: Review declension of ἄνθρωπος and δῶρον.

Our vocabulary words this week are all part of the first declension, but because they end in η, they are declined a little bit differently than the first declension nouns we have already learned.

γραφή	Nominative	γραφαί
γραφῆς	Genitive	γραφῶν
γραφῇ	Dative	γραφαῖς
γραφήν	Accusative	γραφάς

Find the endings on these nouns. Compare this chart to the chart you have for ἀλήθεια. Notice that all the endings in the second column are the same in both charts. In the first column, the only difference is that the −α is changed to an −η. So now we know two sets of first declension endings, and we have found that they really aren't that different from one another. As long as you can remember the rule: *First declension nouns ending in eta keep the eta in all the singular endings*, it is not necessary to memorize the eta-endings in a separate chart. Continue to recite the ἀλήθεια paradigm daily, and do not forget this rule!

day 4: Review conjugation for irregular verb εἰμί.

Today you will translate sentence from English to Greek and from Greek to English. Classify the parts of speech. For nouns, remember to pay attention to case, number and gender. For verbs, consider person and number when you translate.

day 5: Review vocabulary and the alphabet.

α β γ δ ε ζ η θ ι κ λ μ ν ξ ο π ρ σ τ υ φ χ ψ ω

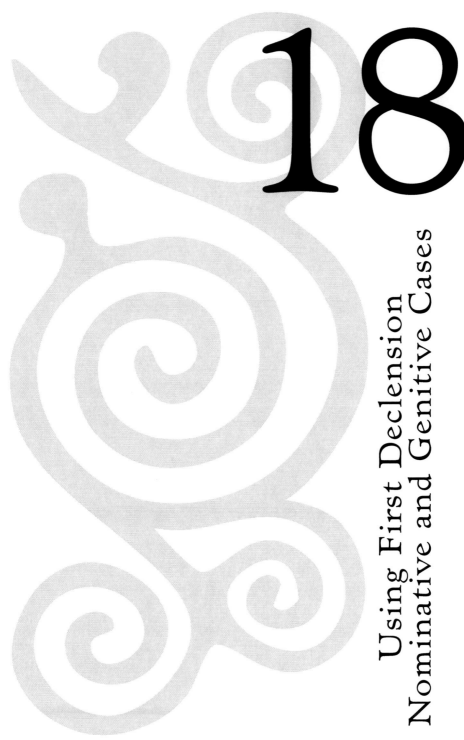

18

Using First Declension Nominative and Genitive Cases

OBJECTIVE: To use both the nominative and genitive cases in translating sentences.

Memory Verse:

Διώκετε τὴν ἀγάπην,
Pursue — *love,*
I Corinthians 14:1a

Spend a few minutes reading through this verse until you are comfortable with pronouncing the words. The very first letter of the very first word is probably unfamiliar to you. This is the uncial form of the letter delta: δ/Δ.*

Look carefully at the first word in the verse. It is a verb. Is there anything about this word that you recognize? You should be able to see that the ending, ετε, is the second person plural ending that you have memorized in your verb conjugation. Even without knowing the meaning of this word, you are still able to see that it is a verb, and that it carries the pronoun *'you'*. (Because it is a command, *you* is implied in the English translation rather than stated.)

day 1 : Review past Memory verses.

Vocabulary:

ἡ φωνή	the voice
ἡ ψυχή	the soul, life
ἡ καρδία	the heart
ἡ ἀγάπη	the love
ἡ ἁμαρτία	the sin

Notice that all your vocabulary words this week are nouns. They are all first declension nouns, so we know that they are feminine nouns. One of these words appears in a declined form in your verse above. Do you know which case the –ην ending in the word ἀγάπην indicates? If you look at the chart you studied last

---

*We use the word *delta* as a geographic term describing the triangular-shaped deposits of land at the mouth of a river.

week (and remember the rule about nouns ending in eta), you will see that it is the accusative singular ending.

Again, this week there are many common derivatives for these words. You will surely be able to think of several of them on your own.

Copy your new verse carefully.

Διώκετε τὴν ἀγάπην,

day 2: Conjugate the verbs πέμπω and βαπτίζω.

Perhaps you remember using the genitive case several weeks ago. In Greek, the genitive case is used to show possession, like our apostrophe-s in English. Today, we are going to begin using the genitive case with our first declension nouns. First go back to your chart and see what the genitive case endings are for first declension nouns. You will remember that the genitive case is on the second line of the chart.

The genitive singular ending is either ας or ης. The genitive plural ending is ων, just like it is for the masculine and neuter second declension nouns. In fact, the genitive plural ending is *always* ων, for any gender noun in the first, second, or third declension. This makes the genitive plural very easy to learn, doesn't it?

Today you are going to practice translating nouns from English into the Greek genitive case. I will use the phrase 'of a...' to show possession.

day 3: Review declensions for ἄνθρωπος, δῶρον, and ἀλήθεια.

You will write the declensions for δῶρον and ἀλήθεια, but say ἄνθρωπος aloud. This should be easy for you. If it is not, then you'll need to remember to read it aloud then say it aloud without looking every day.

Today you will translate some first declension nouns in both the nominative and the genitive case into English. Remember to translate the genitive case with the phrase 'of a...' so that you can see that these nouns are possessive in English as well.

day 4: Review irregular verb εἰμί orally.

Today we will translate sentence from Greek into English. Remember to classify each word as you go.

day 5: Review vocabulary.

19

Sentences Using First and Second Declension Nouns

OBJECTIVE: To be comfortable recognizing and translating first and second declension nouns in sentences.

Memory Verse:

Διώκετε τὴν ἀγάπην,
Pursue — *love,*

I Corinthians 14:1a

day 1: Review past Memory verses.

So far, you have learned six verses in Greek. How many of them are you able to recite from memory?

Vocabulary:

ἡ ἐπαγγελία	the promise
ἡ χαρά	the joy
ὁ Ἰουδαῖος	the Jew
θέλω	I wish
ἁμαρτάνω	I sin

Notice that the word for promise has the same root as ἄγγελος and εὐαγγέλιον. Just as εὐαγγέλιον (the gospel) is a kind of message, so also a promise is a kind of message.

day 2: Conjugate θέλω and ἁμαρτάνω.

Do you remember what purpose noun cases serve? They tell us what job each noun does in the sentence. So far we've learned about the nominative and genitive cases. The nominative case is used as the subject of a sentence (or as the predicate nominative). We find the nominative endings on the first line of our declension charts. The genitive case is used to show possession. We find it on the second line of our declension charts.

day 3: Review declensions for ἄνθρωπος, δῶρον, and ἀλήθεια.

We will do δῶρον orally, and write the others.

Today you will try to translate some sentences from Greek into English. By marking the nouns in the nominative case with an N, the nouns in the genitive case with a G, and the verbs with a V, you will find the sentences much easier to translate. Knowing your endings well will make marking the sentences easier, also.

day 4: Review irregular verb εἰμί.

Today you will translate from English to Greek. Remember to classify your sentences first, marking your subject noun, verbs and possessives. After that, translating should be a breeze!

day 5: Review vocabulary.

20

Article 'The'

OBJECTIVE: To learn how the article adjective 'the' is formed in Greek.

Memory Verse:

Πρόσθες ἡμῖν πίστιν.

Increase   *to us*   *faith.*

Luke 17:5

This is a request that the apostles made of the Lord Jesus Christ: "Increase our faith." It still remains the prayer of all Christan people.

day 1: Review past Memory verses.

Vocabulary: Today we will review vocabulary from past weeks again. Try translating these words into English. Make a note of the ones you do not remember, and spend extra time reviewing them.

ὁ διδάσκαλος

ἡ ἐπαγγελία

τό εὐαγγέλιον

κρίνω

τό πρόσωπον

ἡ χαρά

διδάσκω

τό δῶρον

ἡ εἰρήνη

Once again, copy your verse neatly.

Πρόσθες ἡμῖν πίστιν.

day 2: Conjugate κρίνω and διδάσκω.

You may have noticed that in all the sentences we have translated, we have not used the word 'the' at all. Yet each time you have a noun for a vocabulary word, it always has the word 'the' in front of it. If you have been paying close attention, you have probably even noticed that that word, 'the', in Greek often looks different. In fact, there are 3 different ways you have seen the word spelled. Sometimes it looks like this: ὁ. Sometimes it looks like this: ἡ. And sometimes it looks like this: τό. Maybe you were even observant enough to notice another pattern. Every time we use ἡ for the word 'the', we are talking about a first declension noun. And every time we use ὁ, we are using it with a second declension masculine noun. τό is used with a second declension neuter noun.

Today you will put the correct form of the word 'the' in front of some nouns. Use either ὁ, ἡ, or τό, and remember that the noun and the article (the) must both be the same gender (masculine, feminine, or neuter).

day 3: Write the declensions for δῶρον and ἀλήθεια. Recite the declension for ἄνθρωπος orally.

Now you know that ὁ is the masculine word for 'the' and that it goes with second declension nouns. You also know that ἡ is the first declension feminine word for 'the'. And you know that τό is the neuter word for 'the'. Today you will translate your first sentences with the word 'the'.

day 4: Recite conjugation for irregular verb εἰμί.

Today you will translate sentences in English and in Greek. You will need to remember how to translate the word 'the' and when to use each form.

day 5: Review vocabulary.

21

Nominative and Genitive Case for Article 'The'

OBJECTIVE: To learn how the article adjective 'the' is formed in Greek.

Memory Verse:

Ἀγαπήσεις Κύριον τὸν Θεὸν σου
You shall love   (the) Lord   the   God   of you
Matthew 22:37a

Jesus said that this is the greatest commandment, "You shall love the Lord your God." Do you recognize the uncial forms of α, κ, and θ in the verse above? Also, pay special attention to the ending on σου (ου). Do you recognize this as the genitive ending, causing the word to be translated 'of you'?*

day 1: Review Memory verses.

Vocabulary:

ἐγώ	I
καλύπτω	I hide
ἡ οἰκία	the house
ὁ καρπός	the fruit
ὁ Χριστός	the Messiah, Christ

Today you have a pronoun, a verb, and three nouns in your vocabulary. Can you determine the gender of each of the nouns above? Look carefully at the word οἰκία. Does it remind you of one of your other vocabulary words? οἰκία is a synonym for οἶκος. They both mean 'house', and can be used interchangeably. Just remember that one is feminine and the other is masculine.

---

* Notice that the word ἀγαπήσιες is translated in the future tense. In the future tense, the personal pronoun endings remain the same as they do in the present tense, with the addition of a 'future-tense-sigma', which is inserted between the stem and the ending. Once the student has learned ω, εις, ει, etc., the future tense endings of σω, σεις, σει, σομεν, σετε, σουσι are easily learned. Unfortunately, the future tense is often formed on a different stem than the present tense uses, making the mastery of the tense a bit more difficult.

Write today's verse carefully, as always.

Ἀγαπήσεις Κύριον τὸν Θεὸν σου

day 2: Conjugate the verbs θέλω and φέρω.

Last week we began learning about the word 'the'. There is a lot to learn about this tiny little word, so we are going to be looking at more things this week. We will begin by reviewing what we learned last week. There are 3 forms of 'the' that we have learned. Do you remember what they are? When do we use each one? Do you need to peek at last week's lesson, or do you remember without looking?

In all, we are going to learn 12 of the 24 forms of 'the'. There are six ways to say 'the' in the nominative case—three are singular and three are plural. There are also six ways to say 'the' in the genitive case. (Actually, the genitive plural word for 'the' is always the same, regardless of whether it is masculine, feminine, or neuter. This makes the chart a bit easier to memorize!) These twelve words for 'the' are the twelve forms we will be learning this year. From now on, whenever we use a nominative or a genitive noun, we will be able to use 'the' with it if we want to.

	singular				*plural*		
Masc.	*Fem.*	*Neut.*		*Masc.*	*Fem.*	*Neut.*
ὁ	ἡ	τό	N	οἱ	αἱ	τά
τοῦ	τῆς	τοῦ	G	τῶν	τῶν	τῶν

To read the charts above, read down all four of the masculine articles, and then proceed to the feminine and neuter columns. The only things you need to read aloud are the actual Greek words. Read with me: ὁ, ἡ, τό, τοῦ, τῆς, τοῦ, οἱ, αἱ, τά, τῶν, τῶν, τῶν. Keep practicing this until you know the chart very well. The better you know and understand this chart, the easier it will be for you when we begin adjectives next week.

day 3: Write the declension for ἄνθρωπος and ἀλήθεια. Recite the declension for δῶρον aloud.

Today you will find forms of 'the' on yesterday's chart and identify them by gender, number and case.

day 4: Read through chart for article 'the'.

	singular				plural		
Masc.	Fem.	Neut.			Masc.	Fem.	Neut.
ὁ	ἡ	τό	N		οἱ	αἱ	τά
τοῦ	τῆς	τοῦ	G		τῶν	τῶν	τῶν

The word 'the' must always agree with the word it goes with in gender, number, and case. So, if the noun is a masculine, plural, genitive noun, the word 'the' which goes with it must also be masculine, plural, and genitive.

Today you will write the correct form of 'the' to go with nouns. Before you can select the correct form of 'the', you will need to determine the gender, number and case of each noun. Then translate the words into English.

day 5: Review vocabulary

22

Adjectives

OBJECTIVE : To learn about adjectives and how they are used.

'Αγαπήσεις Κύριον τὸν Θεὸν σου
You shall love   (the) Lord   the   God   of you

ἐν ὅλῃ καρδίᾳ σου
with whole   heart   of you
Matthew 22:37a,b

Remember to work on line two this week. At least one of the words in the new portion of your verse should be familiar to you. Several weeks ago, you learned the word for 'heart' (καρδία). Here, you can see the same word with a dative singular ending. The dative singular ending is easy to recognize because it always has an iota subscript (that little line sitting below the last letter) in the first and second declensions.

day 1 : Recite previous Memory verses.

Vocabulary:

ἀγαθός	good (moral)
ἄλλος	other
ἔσχατος	last
κακός	bad
καλός	good, beautiful

Have you ever heard the theological term *eschatology*? This word refers to the study of end times, or the last days. We also have the word *cacophony*, which uses the Greek words κακός and φωνή to define harsh (or bad) sound. Finally, here is another woman's name for you: *Agatha*. You probably can see which vocabulary word it comes from and what it means.

Write the next portion of your verse neatly.

ἐν ὅλῃ καρδίᾳ σου

day 2: Conjugate σώζω and βαίνω.

Do you know what an adjective is? An adjective is a word that describes a noun. A noun names a person, place, or thing. Boy, horse, garden, clock, and house are all nouns. I could describe each one by adding adjectives to the nouns: **Silly** boy, **swift** horse, **beautiful** garden, **noisy** clock, **large** house. Think of an adjective to add to each of these nouns:

country, cat, father, church, hand, fish, pencil, worm

Look at the vocabulary words you got yesterday. They are all adjectives. They all can be used to describe a noun. As we learn about adjectives, you will see that they have a lot in common with the word 'the', which we were learning about these past few weeks. That is because 'the' is an adjective. It is used so much, that we give it a special name and call it an article.

day 3: Write the declensions for δῶρον and ἀλήθεια. Recite the declension for ἄνθρωπος aloud.

An adjective describes a noun. Just like the word '*the*', there are 24 forms for every adjective. They can be masculine, feminine, neuter…singular, plural…nominative, genitive, dative, or accusative. But just like the word 'the', we will only be learning 12 forms of adjectives for now. An adjective has to change its form to agree with the noun it is describing. If the noun is masculine, plural, and nominative, the adjective must also be masculine, plural, and nominative.

Here is a chart for the adjective ἀγαθός. If you learn this, you will know the endings for many adjectives, because they use the same endings. Read this the same way you read the article chart in last week's lesson.

singular				*plural*		
Masc.	*Fem.*	*Neut.*		*Masc.*	*Fem.*	*Neut.*
ἀγαθός	ἀγαθη	ἀγαθόν	N	ἀγαθοί	ἀγαθαί	ἀγαθά
ἀγαθοῦ	ἀγαθῆς	ἀγαθοῦ	G	ἀγαθῶν	ἀγαθῶν	ἀγαθῶν

Now go back and look at the endings on each adjective above. Did you notice that the genitive plural always has the same ending? Did you also notice that the endings are almost exactly the same as they are for 'the'?

day 4: Read through the chart for 'the' and the chart for adjectives. You will be memorizing these charts.

singular				*plural*		
Masc.	*Fem.*	*Neut.*		*Masc.*	*Fem.*	*Neut.*
ὁ	ἡ	τό	N	οἱ	αἱ	τά
τοῦ	τῆς	τοῦ	G	τῶν	τῶν	τῶν

singular				*plural*		
Masc.	*Fem.*	*Neut.*		*Masc.*	*Fem.*	*Neut.*
ἀγαθός	ἀγαθη	ἀγαθόν	N	ἀγαθοί	ἀγαθαί	ἀγαθά
ἀγαθοῦ	ἀγαθῆς	ἀγαθοῦ	G	ἀγαθῶν	ἀγαθῶν	ἀγαθῶν

Remember that the article or adjective must always agree with the noun in gender, number and case.

day 5: Review vocabulary.

23

Using Adjectives in Sentences

OBJECTIVE: To begin translating sentences including adjectives.

Memory Verse:

’Αγαπήσεις Κύριον τὸν Θεὸν σου
You shall love   (the) Lord   the   God   of you

ἐν ὅλῃ καρδίᾳ σου
with whole   heart   of you

καὶ ἐν ὅλῃ ψυχῇ σου
and   with whole   soul   of you

Matthew 22:37a,b,c

Remember to work on line three this week. Here again you can see a familiar vocabulary word (soul) in the dative case. Notice also that the adjective *whole* (ὅλῃ) which modifies *soul* is in the dative case as well. Adjectives must use the same case as the noun they modify.

day 1: Review past Memory verses.

Vocabulary:

πιστός	faithful
πρῶτος	first
ἅγιος	holy
πονηρός	evil
μικρός	small, little

There are many common derivatives of these vocabulary words. You have likely used a microscope to look (scope) at something small (micro). You have also probably heard of a prototype, or a 'first model'. Did you ever see a picture of the Hagia Sophia? This Byzantine church, whose name means "holy (from ἅγιος) wisdom," was built in Istanbul, Turkey in the 6th century AD.

Write the new phrase for this week's memory verse.

καὶ ἐν ὅλῃ ψυχῇ σου

day 2: Conjugate πιστεύω and καλύπτω.

Today you will orally decline the adjectives from this week's vocabulary into the 12 adjective forms which we are learning. To do this, you will need to learn a rule concerning first declension adjectives and nouns. You have already learned that in first declension nouns, the singular forms can either end in an eta or an alpha. It is the same with adjectives. But how will you decide whether the adjective will use an alpha or an eta, since it is not shown in the words above? First, you need to find the stem by removing the masculine ending from the adjective—so you will remove the –ος.

So πιστός becomes πιστ– and ἅγιος becomes ἅγι–

Then, when you are looking at the stem (the part that is left after you remove the ending) notice what the last letter in the stem is. If it is an ι, ε, or ρ, the feminine ending will use an alpha. If the stem ends with any other letter, the feminine ending will have an eta in the singular forms.

Since the stem for πιστός ends in a τ, the feminine ending will use an eta: πιστή.

Since the stem for ἅγιος ends in a ι, the feminine ending will use an alpha. ἅγια

Now you are ready to decline the adjectives you have learned this week, by removing the –ος and adding the adjective endings you have learned. Remember that only those whose stem ends in ι, ε, or ρ will have an alpha ending. All others will have an eta ending.

day 3: Recite the declensions for the nouns ἄνθρωπος, δῶρον, and ἀλήθεια aloud.

Today you will translate from English to Greek. You have a lot to remember now! If you mark subjects, nouns, possessives, and adjectives in these sentences before you translate them, it will be easier. Remember that articles and adjectives must agree with the nouns they modify in gender, number and case. Choose the case for each noun based on its job within the sentence. Is it the subject? A possessive?

day 4: Read through adjective and article adjective charts.

	singular				*plural*		
	Masc.	*Fem.*	*Neut.*		*Masc.*	*Fem.*	*Neut.*
	ὁ	ἡ	τό	N	οἱ	αἱ	τά
	τοῦ	τῆς	τοῦ	G	τῶν	τῶν	τῶν

singular					*plural*		
Masc.	*Fem.*	*Neut.*			*Masc.*	*Fem.*	*Neut.*
ἀγαθός	ἀγαθή	ἀγαθόν	N		ἀγαθοί	ἀγαθαί	ἀγαθά
ἀγαθοῦ	ἀγαθῆς	ἀγαθοῦ	G		ἀγαθῶν	ἀγαθῶν	ἀγαθῶν

Today you will translate from Greek to English. Look for your verb first. Identify your nouns and the articles and adjectives that agree with them in gender, number and case.

day 5: Review vocabulary.

24

Additional Sentences Using Adjectives

OBJECTIVE : To continue translating
sentences which include adjectives.

Memory Verse:

Ἀγαπήσεις Κύριον τὸν Θεὸν σου
You shall love (the) Lord the God of you

ἐν ὅλῃ καρδίᾳ σου
with whole heart of you

καὶ ἐν ὅλῃ ψυχῇ σου
and with whole soul of you

καὶ ἐν ὅλῃ τῇ διανοίᾳ σου.
and with whole the mind of you.

Matthew 22:37

Remember to work on the final line this week. By the end of this week, you should know this entire verse, which in English is commonly written, "You shall love the Lord your God with all your heart, with all your soul, and with all your mind."

day 1 : Review past Memory verses.

Vocabulary:

δίκαιος	righteous
νεκρός	dead
δεύτερος	second
ὁ Φαρισαῖος	the Pharisee
ἀποστέλλω	I send

Notice that three of your vocabulary words are adjectives. Will these take alpha or eta in their feminine singular endings? Do you remember the rule? *If the stem ends in ε, ι, or ρ, the feminine singular ending begins with alpha.*

Also look at the only verb in the list above, ἀποστέλλω. Did you notice how similar it is to the word ἀπόστολος? They share the same root. Remember that an apostle is *one who is sent*.

Can you name the fifth book of the Bible, in the Old Testament? This book is called *Deuteronomy*, or *Second Law*. As you can see, the title of the book comes from two Greek words you have studied, δεύτερος and νόμος

Write the last phrase of Matthew 22:37.

κατ ἐν ὅλῃ τῇ διανοίᾳ σου.

day 2: Conjugate ἀποστέλλω and λύω.

Today you will work on making sure nouns and adjectives agree in gender, number, and case. I will give you a noun phrase, and you will add an adjective, making sure that it is in the correct form. Let's start with ἡ ζωή, 'the life'. The article and noun have the same gender, number and case: feminine, singular and nominative. Now let's add an adjective, δίκαιος, righteous. We need to make it feminine, singular and nominative as well. First, we find the stem by dropping the −ος: δίκαι−. Now, we need to decide if the feminine ending will have an alpha or an eta. Do you remember our rule? If the stem ends in an ι, ε, or ρ, the feminine ending will use an alpha. So this time, we will use an alpha ending. The feminine, singular, nominative ending for δίκαιος is δίκαια. So our whole phrase becomes ἡ δίκαια ζωή.

Follow these same steps as you add adjectives to the noun-phrases in your workbook today. Make your adjectives agree in gender, number and case. If you need a feminine ending, decide whether you should use an alpha or eta ending. Write the phrase.

day 3: Recite the declensions for ἄνθρωπος, δῶρον, and ἀλήθεια.

Today you will classify sentences and translate from English to Greek. See if you can remember the steps to classify and translate your sentences on your own. You've sure had lots of practice!

day 4: Read through declensions for 'the' and the adjective ἀγαθός.

singular				*plural*		
Masc.	*Fem.*	*Neut.*		*Masc.*	*Fem.*	*Neut.*
ὁ	ἡ	τό	N	οἱ	αἱ	τά
τοῦ	τῆς	τοῦ	G	τῶν	τῶν	τῶν

singular				*plural*		
Masc.	*Fem.*	*Neut.*		*Masc.*	*Fem.*	*Neut.*
ἀγαθός	ἀγαθή	ἀγαθόν	N	ἀγαθοί	ἀγαθαί	ἀγαθά
ἀγαθοῦ	ἀγαθῆς	ἀγαθοῦ	G	ἀγαθῶν	ἀγαθῶν	ἀγαθῶν

Today we will translate from Greek to English.

day 5: Review vocabulary.

25

Prepositions With the Genitive

OBJECTIVE : To begin learning how
prepositional phrases are formed in Greek.

Ἀγαπήσεις τὸν πλησίον σου
You shall love   the   neighbor   of you
Matthew 22:39

For the past several weeks you have been learning the commandment that Jesus says is the greatest commandment: "You shall love the Lord your God with all your heart, with all your soul, and with all your mind." He goes on to say that the second greatest commandment is, "You shall love your neighbor as yourself." As you can see, that is the verse you will be working on for the next few weeks.

day 1: Review past Memory verses.

Vocabulary:

ἀπό (with the genitive)   from

διά (with the genitive)   through

ἐκ/ἐξ (with the genitive)   out of

μετά (with the genitive)   with

κατά (with the genitive)   against

The word ἐκ changes its form to ἐξ when the next word begins with a vowel. These words are all prepositions. This week we will be learning what prepositions are and how they are used in Greek.

Copy this week's verse.

Ἀγαπήσεις τὸν πλησίον σου

day 2: Conjugate πιστεύω and εἰμί.
Remember that εἰμί is an irregular verb.

A preposition is a word that connects a noun to a sentence. Here is a sentence:

> Mary sat.

Here is a noun:

> chair

If I want to connect chair to the sentence I gave you, I will use a preposition.

> Mary sat **on** the chair.
> Mary sat **under** the chair.
> Mary sat **beside** the chair.

There are many, many prepositions. Perhaps you have memorized a list of them for your English lessons. In a sentence, prepositions always have a noun that comes after them. That noun is called the *object of the preposition*. In Greek, the object of the preposition must be in a certain case. Some prepositions must have their object in the genitive case, and some have objects in the accusative and dative cases. Sometimes a preposition takes more than one case for its object, but then its meaning changes depending on the case used. All of the prepositions you are learning right now take the genitive case. When you are learning the prepositions, you must learn the case that their object takes along with the preposition itself. So do not think that it is enough to know that μετά means *with*. You must know that μετά-with-the-genitive means *with*. Right now, this may seem silly to you, since all of your prepositions are with-the-genitive. But when you begin learning additional prepositions, you will be glad that you memorized these in this way.

Here is a sentence:

> The man is with the apostle.

'Man' will be in the nominative case because it is the subject of the sentence. (Who is the sentence about? Man.)

'Is' is the verb.

'With' is the preposition.

'Apostle', the object of the preposition, is in the genitive case.

ὁ ἄνθρωπός ἐστι μετὰ τοῦ ἀποστόλου.

The man   is   with the   apostle.

day 3: Write the declensions for ἄνθρωπος, δῶρον, and ἀλήθεια.

Today you will translate prepositional phrases from English to Greek. Remember that the object of the preposition must be translated with the case ending that goes with that particular preposition. All of our prepositions so far use the genitive case, so you will give your objects genitive endings.

day 4: Read aloud the 12 forms of adjectives and the word 'the'.

singular				*plural*		
Masc.	*Fem.*	*Neut.*		*Masc.*	*Fem.*	*Neut.*
ὁ	ἡ	τό	N	οἱ	αἱ	τά
τοῦ	τῆς	τοῦ	G	τῶν	τῶν	τῶν

singular				*plural*		
Masc.	*Fem.*	*Neut.*		*Masc.*	*Fem.*	*Neut.*
ἀγαθός	ἀγαθή	ἀγαθόν	N	ἀγαθοί	ἀγαθαί	ἀγαθά
ἀγαθοῦ	ἀγαθῆς	ἀγαθοῦ	G	ἀγαθῶν	ἀγαθῶν	ἀγαθῶν

Today you will classify and translate sentences from English to Greek. Pay careful attention to your prepositional phrases.

day 5: Review vocabulary.

26

Using Prepostions

OBJECTIVE: To continue learning how
prepositional phrases are formed in Greek.

Memory Verse:

Ἀγαπήσεις τὸν πλησίον σου
You shall love   the   neighbor   of you

ὡς σεαυτόν.
as   yourself.

Matthew 22:39

You may find the final word in this verse a little difficult to pronounce. Remember that αυ is a diphthong and pronounce this word with three syllables:

σε   αυ   τον.

day 1 : Review past Memory verses.

Vocabulary:

ἡ ἔρημος	the desert
ἡ ὁδός	the road, the way
πρό (with gen)	before
παρά (with gen)	from
περί (with gen)	about

Did you notice something unusual about your first two vocabulary words? Notice that they are both nouns that end in ος. Nouns that end in ος are second declension nouns. Second declension nouns are either masculine or neuter. **But,** these nouns have the word ἡ for 'the'. ἡ is the feminine word for 'the'. What does that mean? That means that these two words are rule breakers. They are feminine nouns, and they break the rule that says: *second declension nouns ending in ος are masculine*. Even though they are feminine, they are declined the same way as masculine second declension nouns.

Write this week's phrase.

ὡς σεαυτόν.

day 2: Conjugate ἀποστέλλω and εἰμί.

Remember that εἰμί is an irregular verb.

Remember that ἔρημος and ὁδός are second-declension rule-breakers. They are feminine nouns, but they are declined just like masculine nouns. When using these words in your translation exercises, you must remember to use the correct form of *the* with them. Because these are feminine words, they always take the feminine form of the article. Up until now, the endings on your articles and the endings on the nouns they modify have always been very similar: τοῦ ἀνθρώπου, αἱ ἀλήθειαι, τό πλοῖον... but notice how these two words, because they are exceptions to the gender rule, do not have endings that match the endings on their articles: τῆς ὁδοῦ, αἱ ἔρημοι.

day 3: Recite the declensions for ἄνθρωπος, δῶρον, and ἀλήθεια.

Do you remember what a preposition is? A preposition joins a noun to a sentence. This week, you have three new prepositions. They all go with nouns in the genitive case.

day 4: Recite 12 forms of adjectives and the word 'the'.

	singular					*plural*		
	Masc.	*Fem.*	*Neut.*			*Masc.*	*Fem.*	*Neut.*
	ὁ	ἡ	τό	N		οἱ	αἱ	τά
	τοῦ	τῆς	τοῦ	G		τῶν	τῶν	τῶν

	singular					*plural*		
	Masc.	*Fem.*	*Neut.*			*Masc.*	*Fem.*	*Neut.*
	ἀγαθός	ἀγαθή	ἀγαθόν	N		ἀγαθοί	ἀγαθαί	ἀγαθά
	ἀγαθοῦ	ἀγαθῆς	ἀγαθοῦ	G		ἀγαθῶν	ἀγαθῶν	ἀγαθῶν

Your translation exercises today include prepositional phrases. Remember that the object of the preposition must be in a particular case, depending on the preposition used.

day 5: Review vocabulary.

27

Prepositions in Sentences

OBJECTIVE : To continue learning how prepositional phrases are formed in Greek.

Memory Verse:

Πάτερ ἡμῶν ὁ ἐν τοῖς οὐρανοῖς,
Father   of us   the one in the   heavens,
Matthew 6:9a

day 1 : Review past Memory verses.

You're nearing the end of Greek 1! Today you'll take a mini vocabulary quiz to see how much you remember from your year. How many of the words do you remember? Do you know what part of speech they are? (noun, verb, adjective, preposition, etc.)

Write this week's memory verse. Do you recognize some of the words and forms?

Πάτερ ἡμῶν ὁ ἐν τοῖς οὐρανοῖς,

day 2 : Conjugate ἄγω and φέρω orally.

Today you will classify some Greek sentences and parse the nouns as you go. Find the nouns first (*N*), and mark them with gender (use *m, f,* or *n*), number (*s* or *p*), and case (*n* for nominative and *g* for genitive). Then mark verbs (*V*), articles (*art*) and prepositions (*prep*). For example:

art	*N:m/s/n*	*art*	*N:m/s/g*	*V*	*prep*	*art*	*N:m/s/g*
ὁ	ἄγγελος	τοῦ	θεοῦ	μένει	μετά	τοῦ	ἀνθρώπου.

day 3: Recite the declensions for ἄνθρωπος, δῶρον, and ἀλήθεια.

Today you will translate sentences from yesterday into English.

day 4: Recite 12 forms of adjectives and the word 'the'.

Today we will translate sentences from English to Greek. Think about proper endings for each word.

day 5: Review vocabulary.

28

Review

OBJECTIVE: To review vocabulary and sentence construction.

Memory Verse:

Πάτερ ἡμῶν ὁ   ἐν τοῖς οὐρανοῖς,
Father   of us   the   one in the   heavens,

Ἁγιασθήτω τὸ ὄνομά σου.
Let it be hallowed   the   name   of you.

Matthew 6:9

day 1 : Review past Memory verses.

Today you will take another vocabulary quiz. How well have you learned the words we've practiced all year?

day 2 : Conjugate ἀκούω and εἰμί in your workbook.

Do you remember the word we used to describe what kind of language Greek is? We said it is an *inflected* language. Do you remember what this means? It means that the endings on the words tell us what job each word has in the sentence. Because of this, the words can sometimes get a little mixed up compared to the way we put them in English sentences. Look at your new Memory verse above. Notice how things look a little mixed up when we just write the English words under each Greek word. After we translate each word, we have to rearrange the sentence so it makes sense to us. Remember that it looks mixed up because Greek is an *inflected* language.

In an inflected language, words must be *conjugated* and *declined*. Verbs are conjugated with different personal endings, and nouns and adjectives are declined to show their gender, number, and case. In the list of vocabulary words above, indicate whether each word should be conjugated or declined.

day 3: Write the declensions for ἄνθρωπος, δῶρον, and ἀλήθεια in your workbook.

Classify the Greek sentences in your workbook today, and parse the nouns as you go. Mark nouns first (N), then identify their gender (use *m, f,* or *n*), number (*s* or *p*), and case (*n* for nominative and *g* for genitive). Then mark verbs (*V*), articles (*art*) and prepositions (*prep*). For example:

art	*N:m/s/n*	*art*	*N:m/s/g*	*V*	*prep*	*art*	*N:m/s/g*
ὁ	ἄγγελος	τοῦ	θεοῦ	μένει	μετά	τοῦ	ἀνθρώπου.

day 4: Write 12 forms of adjectives and 'the' in your workbook.

Today you will translate the sentences you classified yesterday.

day 5: Review vocabulary.

29

Review

OBJECTIVE : To review vocabulary and sentence construction.

Review vocabulary and memory verses today. You've learned a lot this year!

day 1: Review past Memory verses.

Take another vocabulary quiz. Can you remember all the words quickly and easily?
Can you identify the part of speech?

day 2: Conjugate γινώσκω and ἄγω in your workbook.

Remember that in Greek, the personal pronoun is *part of* the verb. Personal
pronouns are: I, you, he, she, it, we, you, they. In Greek, they are found in the
conjugation endings. Because these are part of the verb, we do not need to use
separate words for them.

day 3: Recite the declensions for ἄνθρωπος, δῶρον, and ἀλήθεια.

Classify Greek sentences in your workbook.

day 4: Write 12 forms of the adjective ἀγαθός and the word 'the'.

Today you will translate the sentences you classified yesterday.

day 5: Review vocabulary.

30

Review

OBJECTIVE: To review vocabulary and sentence construction.

day 1 : Review past Memory verses.

This is your final vocabulary quiz. How well have you learned the words we've studied this year?

day 2 : Conjugate βαίνω and γράφω in your workbook.

Remember that every noun has a special ending which shows its gender, number, and case. Can you explain what the words *gender*, *number*, and *case* mean?

day 3 : Recite the declensions for ἄνθρωπος, δῶρον, and ἀλήθεια.

What is an adjective? Remember that an adjective is a word that describes a noun. We know that nouns must have a gender, number, and case. It is also important to remember that adjectives must **agree** with nouns. That means that they must have the same gender, number, and case as the noun has.

day 4 : Write 12 forms of the adjective ἀγαθός and the word 'the' in your workbook.

Today you will classify and translate English sentences into Greek. These are difficult sentences, but you have learned a lot this year.

day 5: Review vocabulary.

Well done! You have completed your first year of Greek study! You have learned over 100 vocabulary words, ten Memory verses, and several important grammatical concepts.

Appendix A: Greek-English Glossary

ἀγαθός	good (moral)	*Agatha*
ἀγάπη, ἡ	love	
ἄγγελος, ὁ	messenger, angel	*angel*
ἅγιος	holy	*Hagia Sophia*
ἀγρός, ὁ	field	*agriculture*
ἄγω	I lead	
ἀδελφός, ὁ	brother	*Philadelphia*
ἀκούω	I hear	*acoustic*
ἀλήθεια, ἡ	truth	
ἄλλος	other	*alien*
ἁμαρτάνω	I sin	
ἁμαρτία, ἡ	sin	
ἁμαρτωλός, ὁ	sinner	
ἄνθρωπος, ὁ	man	*anthropology*
ἀπό(with gen)	from	*apology*
ἀποστέλλω	I send	
ἀπόστολος, ὁ	apostle	*apostle*
ἄρτος, ὁ	bread	
βαίνω	I go	
βάλλω	I throw	*ballistic*
βαπτίζω	I baptize	*baptize*
βασιλεία, ἡ	kingdom	*basil, basilica*
βίος, ὁ	life	*biology*
βιβλίον, τό	book	*Bible, bibliography*
βλέπω	I see	
γινώσκω	I know	*know, gnostic*
γραφή, ἡ	writing, Scripture	*graph, graphic*
γράφω	I write	*graphite*
δαιμόνιον, τό	demon	*demon*

δέκα	ten	*decade*
δεύτερος	second	*Deuteronomy*
διά (with gen)	through	*diameter*
διδάσκαλος, ὁ	teacher	
διδάσκω	I teach	*didactic*
δίκαιος	righteous	
δοῦλος, ὁ	slave	
δῶρον, τό	gift	
ἐγείρω	I raise up	
ἐγώ	I	*ego*
εἰρήνη, ἡ	peace	*Irene, irenic*
ἐκ/ἐξ (with gen)	out of	*exit*
ἐκκλησία, ἡ	church	*ecclesiastical*
ἐντολη, ἡ	commandment	
ἐπαγγελία, ἡ	promise	
ἔργον, τό	work	*erg, ergonomic*
ἔρημος, ἡ	desert	*hermit*
ἔσχατος	last	*eschatology*
εὐαγγέλιον, τό	gospel	*evangelical*
ἔχω	I have or hold	
ζωή, ἡ	life	*zoo, zoology*
ἡμέρα, ἡ	day	
θάνατος, ὁ	death	*Thanatopsis, euthanasia*
θέλω	I wish	
θεός, ὁ	God	*theology*
ἱερόν, τό	temple	
᾽Ιησοῦς	Jesus	
᾽Ιουδαῖος, ὁ	Jew	
καί	and	

Greek	English	Derivative
κακός	bad	*cacophony*
καλός	good, beautiful	*kaleidoscope*
καλύπτω	I hide	
καρδία, ἡ	heart	*cardiologist*
καρπός, ὁ	fruit	
κατά (with gen)	against	*cataclysm*
κόσμος, ὁ	world	*cosmos, cosmic*
κρίνω	I judge	
κύριος, ὁ	lord	
λαμβάνω	I take	
λέγω	I say or speak	*legend*
λίθος, ὁ	stone	*lithography, monolith*
λόγος, ὁ	word	*theology, biology, etc*
λύω	I loose or destroy	
μένω	I remain	*remain*
μετά (with gen)	with	*metaphor*
μικρός	small, little	*microscope, microbe*
νεκρός	dead	*necrosis*
νόμος, ὁ	law	*Deuteronomy*
ὁδός, ἡ	road, way	*exodus*
οἰκία, ἡ	house	
οἶκος, ὁ	house	
οὐρανός, ὁ	heaven	*uranium*
παρά (with gen)	from	*paramedic*
παραβολή, ἡ	parable	*parable*
πάσχω	I suffer	
πέμπω	I send	
περί (with gen)	about	*perimeter*
πιστεύω	I believe	*epistemology*
πιστός	faithful	
πλοῖον, τό	boat	
πονηρός	evil	

πρό (with gen)	before	*prologue*
πρόσωπον, τό	face	
πρῶτος	first	*prototype*
σώζω	I save	
τέκνον, τό	child	
τόπος, ὁ	place	*topography, topology*
τυφλός, ὁ	blind man	
υἱός, ὁ	son	
Φαρισαῖος, ὁ	Pharisee	*Pharisee*
φέρω	I bear, bring	
φωνή, ἡ	voice	*telephone, phonograph*
χαρά, ἡ	joy	*charismatic*
Χριστός, ὁ	Messiah, Christ	*Christ*
ψυχή, ἡ	soul, life	*psychiatrist, psychology*
ὥρα, ἡ	hour	*hour*

Appendix B: English-Greek Glossary

about	περί (with gen)
against	κατά (with gen)
and	καί
apostle	ἀπόστολος, ὁ
bad	κακός
baptize, I	βαπτίζω
bear, I	φέρω
before	πρό (with gen)
believe, I	πιστεύω
blind man	τυφλός, ὁ
boat	πλοῖον, τό
book	βιβλίον, τό
bread	ἄρτος, ὁ
brother	ἀδελφός, ὁ
child	τέκνον, τό
church	ἐκκλησία, ἡ
commandment	ἐντολή, ἡ
day	ἡμέρα, ἡ
dead	νεκρός
death	θάνατος, ὁ
demon	δαιμόνιον, τό
desert	ἔρημος, ἡ
evil	πονηρός
face	πρόσωπον, τό
faithful	πιστός
field	ἀγρός, ὁ
first	πρῶτος
from	ἀπό (with gen)
from	παρά (with gen)
fruit	καρπός, ὁ

gift	δῶρον, τό
go, I	βαίνω
God	θεός, ὁ
good (beautiful)	καλός
good (moral)	ἀγαθός
gospel	εὐαγγέλιον, τό
have, I	ἔχω
hear, I	ἀκούω
heart	καρδία, ἡ
heaven	οὐρανός, ὁ
hide, I	καλύπτω
holy	ἅγιος
hour	ὥρα, ἡ
house	οἰκία, ἡ
house	οἶκος, ὁ
I	ἐγώ
Jesus	Ἰησοῦς
Jew	Ἰουδαῖος
joy	χαρά, ἡ
judge, I	κρίνω
kingdom	βασιλεία, ἡ
know, I	γινώσκω
last	ἔσχατος
law	νόμος, ὁ
lead, I	ἄγω
life	βίος, ὁ
life	ζωή, ἡ
loose, I	λύω
lord	κύριος, ὁ
love	ἀγάπη, ἡ
man	ἄνθρωπος, ὁ
messenger, angel	ἄγγελος, ὁ
Messiah, Christ	Χριστός, ὁ

other	ἄλλος
out of	ἐκ/ἐξ (with gen)
parable	παραβολή, ἡ
peace	εἰρήνη, ἡ
Pharisee	Φαρισαῖος, ὁ
place	τόπος, ὁ
promise	ἐπαγγελία, ἡ
raise up, I	ἐγείρω
remain, I	μένω
righteous	δίκαιος
road, way	ὁδός, ἡ
save, I	σῴζω
say, I	λέγω
second	δεύτερος
see, I	βλέπω
send, I	ἀποστέλλω
send, I	πέμπω
sin	ἁμαρτία, ἡ
sin, I	ἁμαρτάνω
sinner	ἁμαρτωλός, ὁ
slave	δοῦλος, ὁ
small, little	μικρός
son	υἱός, ὁ
soul, life	ψυχή, ἡ
stone	λίθος, ὁ
suffer, I	πάσχω
take, I	λαμβάνω
teach, I	διδάσκω
teacher	διδάσκαλος, ὁ
temple	ἱερόν, τό
ten	δέκα
through	διά (with gen)
throw, I	βάλλω
truth	ἀλήθεια, ἡ

voice	φωνή, ἡ
wish, I	θέλω
with	μετά (with gen)
work	ἔργον, τό
world	κόσμος, ὁ
word	λόγος, ὁ
write, I	γράφω
writing, Scripture	γραφή, ἡ

Appendix C: Memory Verses

Ἐν ἀρχῇ ἦν ὁ Λόγος, καὶ ὁ Λόγος ἦν πρὸς τὸν Θεόν,
καὶ Θεὸς ἦν ὁ λόγος.
In (the) beginning was the word, and the word was with the God, and God
was the word.
John 1:1

Ἐγώ εἰμι ἡ ὁδὸς καὶ ἡ ἀλήθεια καὶ ἡ ζωή·
I am the way and the truth and the life;
John 14:6

Νυνὶ δὲ μένει πίστις, ἐλπίς, ἀγάπη,
τὰ τρία ταῦτα·
μείζων δὲ τούτων ἡ ἀγάπη.
And now remain faith, hope, and love,
these three;
but the greatest of these is love.
I Corinthians 13:13

Πάντοτε χαίρετε
Always rejoice
I Thessalonians 5:16

"Ἐγώ εἰμι τὸ Ἄλφα καὶ τὸ Ὦ,"
Λέγει Κύριος ὁ Θεός,
Ὁ ὢν καὶ ὁ ἦν καὶ ὁ ἐρχόμενος,
Ὁ Παντοκράτωρ.
"I am the Alpha and the Omega,"
says the Lord,
Who is and who was and who is to come,
The Almighty.
Revelation 1:8

Διώκετε τὴν ἀγάπην,
Pursue love,
I Corinthians 14:1a

Πρόσθες ἡμῖν πίστιν.
Increase our faith.
Luke 17:5

Ἀγαπήσεις Κύριον τὸν Θεὸν σου
ἐν ὅλῃ καρδίᾳ σου
καὶ ἐν ὅλῃ ψυχῇ σου
καὶ ἐν ὅλῃ τῇ διανοίᾳ σου.
You shall love the Lord your God
with all your heart
and with all your soul
and with all your mind.
Matthew 22:37

Ἀγαπήσεις τὸν πλησίον σου
ὡς σεαυτόν.
You shall love your neighbor
as yourself.
Matthew 22:39

Πάτερ ἡμῶν ὁ ἐν τοῖς οὐρανοῖς,
Ἁγιασθήτω τὸ ὄνομά σου.
Our Father in heaven,
Hallowed be your name.
Matthew 6:9

Appendix D: Reference Charts

The Greek Alphabet

α	β	γ	δ	ε	ζ
A	B	Γ	Δ	E	Z
alpha	beta	gamma	delta	epsilon	zeta

η	θ	ι	κ	λ	μ
H	Θ	I	K	Λ	M
eta	theta	iota	kappa	lambda	mu

ν	ξ	ο	π	ρ	σ , ς
N	Ξ	O	Π	P	Σ
nu	xi	omicron	pi	rho	sigma

τ	υ	φ	χ	ψ	ω
T	Υ	Φ	X	Ψ	Ω
tau	upsilon	phi	chi	psi	omega

Present Tense Verb Endings

−ω	−ομεν
−εις	−ετε
−ει	−ουσι

Second Declension Case Endings (Masculine)

singular		plural	
—ος	N	—οι	
—ου	G	—ων	
—ῳ	D	—οις	
—ον	A	—ους	

Second Declension Case Endings (Neuter)

singular		plural	
—ον	N	—α	
—ου	G	—ων	
—ῳ	D	—οις	
—ον	A	—α	

Irregular Verb εἰμί

εἰμί	ἐσμέν
εἶ	ἐστέ
ἐστί	εἰσί

First Declension Case Endings (Feminine)

singular		plural	
—α/η	N	—αι	
—ας/ης	G	—ων	
—ᾳ/ῃ	D	—αις	
—αν/ην	A	—ας	

Article 'the'

singular

Masc.	Fem.	Neut.		Masc.	Fem.	Neut.
ὁ	ἡ	τό	N	οἱ	αἱ	τά
τοῦ	τῆς	τοῦ	G	τῶν	τῶν	τῶν

plural

Adjectives

singular

Masc.	Fem.	Neut.		Masc.	Fem.	Neut.
ἀγαθός	ἀγαθή	ἀγαθόν	N	ἀγαθοί	ἀγαθαί	ἀγαθά
ἀγαθοῦ	ἀγαθῆς	ἀγαθοῦ	G	ἀγαθῶν	ἀγαθῶν	ἀγαθῶν

plural

Appendix E: Grammar Review

In many ways, Greek is similar to English. The purpose of this review is to draw attention to these similarities, and also to further explain the areas where Greek and English grammar differ.

To begin with, Greek and English have the same parts of speech.

A **noun** is a naming word. It names a person, place, thing, or idea. Some examples of nouns are: *boat, faith, grass, nose, man, village.*

A **pronoun** is a word that replaces a noun. *He, she, we,* and *they* are some pronouns. These words can be substituted for nouns in various parts of the sentence. Greek has pronouns, though they are not covered in this course. However, the Greek pronoun-endings (part of all Greek verbs) are explained and used.

An **adjective** describes a noun. It answers the questions "Which one," "How many," or "What kind?" *Small, ten, many, red,* and *pretty* are all adjectives.

An **article** is really an adjective, but it is so common that it has the name *article* to distinguish it from the rest of the adjectives. There are three articles in English (*a, an, the*), but in Greek there is only one (*the*).

A **verb** is a word that shows action or being. The words *run, think, read, slither,* and *believe* are all actions. The being verbs are *am, is, are, was, were, be, being,* and *been.* In this course, we only learn verbs in the present tense.

A **preposition** is a word that joins a noun (called the object of the preposition) to a sentence. A preposition expresses relationship. *Under, about, through,* and *with* are prepositions. *A man goes* under *a bridge. The girl thinks* about *the book.*

These are the basic parts of speech which are introduced in this course. The higher your comfort level with English grammar, the easier it will be for you to understand Greek grammar.

In English, our understanding is based largely on the position a word has in the sentence. *The boy loves the dog* and *The dog loves the boy* express two completely different thoughts. In the first sentence, *boy* is the subject. It comes before the verb, and it answers the question "Who loves?" When the position of the words changes, the answer to the question "Who loves?" also changes. In the second sentence, *dog* is the subject. If I say, *The young boy loves the dog*, I know that the boy is young because the word *young* precedes the word *boy*. Notice how the meaning changes when we move the word *young*: *The boy loves the* young *dog*.

While the Greek language is fully capable of expressing these same ideas, it does not use word position to do so. Greek, like Latin, is an **inflected** language. This means that the language has a system of word endings which are used to show the part a word plays in a sentence. Word order is not as important in Greek. The *endings* are the clues to syntax. A student of Greek is in some ways like a detective, becoming aware of these clues and finding them in the sentence.

Greek nouns have five cases. The cases show the different functions the noun can have in a sentence. Below, the cases are listed with their principal functions.

Nominative	Subject/ Predicate nominative
Genitive	Possessive (key word *of*)
Dative	Indirect object (key words *to/for*)
Accusative	Direct object
(Vocative	Direct address)*

My students regularly chant through a simplified version of this chart to help them remember the noun functions and their cases. The simplified version looks like this:

Nominative	Subject
Genitive	*of a*
Dative	*to/for*
Accusative	DO

Each of the cases listed above has its own singular ending and its own plural ending. Listing a noun with all of its endings is called **declining** the noun. In this

---

* The vocative case is not covered in this course. In the sentence, "Mary, please close the door," the word *Mary* would be in the vocative case, because it indicates the person to whom the sentence is directed. Because the vocative has the same ending as the nominative in most declensions and genders, it is unnecessary to learn it as a separate ending.

course, complete declensions are learned, although only the first two cases are studied in terms of their functions.

Greek has three declensions. (The first two declensions are covered this year.) Each of the declensions has its own set of endings. There are some similarities between the endings, and these are noted in the text to aid in memorization. The declensions as they are taught in this course are listed in Appendix D.

Greek verbs have their own endings as well. The verb endings differ from the noun endings, and they show the person and number to which the verb refers. An easy way to understand this is to think of the verb ending as equivalent to an English pronoun. The English phrase *We think* is shown by a single word in Greek which is made of two parts—the **stem**, which expresses the idea *think* + the **ending**, which indicates the personal pronoun *we*. The ending changes when the pronoun changes. Writing a verb with all of its endings is called **conjugating** the verb. In this course, only the present indicative conjugation is learned. It also is listed in Appendix D.

This is Greek grammar in its most simplistic terms. Now, let's look at a few examples of how this works. In these examples, diagrams and word classification are used to give a better picture of the different functions. These are important tools and should be used throughout the course to aid the student in the translation exercises.

Example 1:

> *A man eats.*

> First, we identify the subject, verb, and any other words in the sentence. Asking "Who or what is the sentence about?" shows that *man* is the subject. The subject is written on the first horizontal line in a diagram. Next, we ask, "What does the man do?" The answer is, "He eats," so *eats* is the verb in this sentence. The verb is located next to the subject on the diagram, after a vertical line. The only other word left in this sentence is *a*, which is an article, and is located below *man* in the diagram.

> *article subject verb*
> A   man   eats.

Now, we can look at this sentence again, and determine which Greek word we will use for each of these words. I will begin with the word *man*, the subject of this sentence. Above, we listed subject as the function of the nominative case, so I know that *man* will have the nominative ending. The ending will also be singular, because we are talking about one man, not many men. In this case, the ending will be –ος. The nominative case tells us that this word is the subject of the sentence, so I can put this word first, last, or in the middle of the sentence. No matter where it is, it will always be the subject.

Remember that in Greek there is no word for *a*. This word is not translated.

The word *eats* is the verb. Because we need to include the pronoun ending in Greek, we can think of it as *he eats*. The present indicative ending for *he* (3rd person singular) is –ει.

ἄνθρωπος ἐσθίει.

ἐσθίει ἄνθρωπος.

These sentences both say the same thing.

Example 2:

The first son of a teacher believes.

Here again, we begin by asking our standard questions to determine who the sentence is about and what he is doing (subject and verb). Next, we see that the words *the* and *first* modify our subject by answering the question, "Which son?" On the diagram, they are located on slanted lines below the subject. Notice also that one of our key words is in this sentence. The word *of* should immediately make us think of the genitive case. The whole phrase *of a teacher* is translated by the single word *teacher* with the genitive (*of a*) ending.

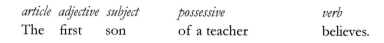

	article	*adjective*	*subject*	*possessive*	*verb*
	The	first	son	of a teacher	believes.

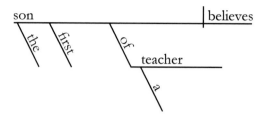

The subject will be in the nominative case. Any articles or adjectives take the same case as the word they modify. That means that *the* and *first* are in the nominative case as well. We have already noted that the phrase *of a teacher* is in the genitive case. *Believes*, or *he believes*, takes the 3rd person singular ending.

ὁ πρῶτος υἱὸς διδασκάλου πιστεύει.
The first   son   of a teacher   (he) teaches.

Here the sentence order looks very much like a typical English sentence. But remember, we can change the sentence order around and still say the same thing.

πιστεύει ὁ πρῶτος υἱὸς διδασκάλου.

πιστεύει διδασκάλου ὁ πρῶτος υἱὸς.

Appendix F: Review activities

Your success in mastering Greek is largely based on how well you memorize the various aspects of the language as you learn them. The lessons are set up with review exercises or reminders built in to the different days (Memory verses on day one, verbs on day two, nouns on day three, and adjectives on day four). You may have noticed already that the fifth day of every lesson is wholly devoted to vocabulary review. Use day five to go over the current lesson's vocabulary, and to pull in vocabulary from previous lessons. Also, if extra review is needed with any of the verb/noun charts or memory verses, day five is a good time to do this. In this section, you will find several suggestions for review, including games and drill work. Hopefully, these ideas will be both fun and profitable for you.

Put flashcards to good use. Because they are portable, they are easy to use in odd moments—in the car, waiting at the dentist, in line at the grocery store. We just grab them on the way out the door.

In memorizing vocabulary, some students find it useful to know an English derivative for the word. While many derivatives are discussed in the chapters, additional ones are listed in the vocabulary lists at the back of the book. Use these if they are helpful for your child.

The "Memory" matching game is a wonderfully simple and effective way to review alphabet and vocabulary. It is easy to make up matches that have the alphabet symbol on one card and the name of the letter on the other card. For vocabulary review in later lessons, the matches would consist of English on one card and Greek on another. We have made a practice of playing Memory every Friday for our vocabulary review. Not only do the children find it fun, but they get a lot of practice reading the Greek words and translating them. Other simple card games, such as "Go Fish" and "Old Maid," work well as vocabulary review.

Transliteration activities are an excellent way to practice using the sounds and letters of the Greek alphabet. Try writing a note to your student using Greek letters. Have your student reply with his own transliterated response. The Greek alphabet makes a great secret code!

Each time a new chart is presented for memorization, you will find it worthwhile to require your student to write the chart out several times. This is a quick and easy way to ensure that the student masters the content of the chart. I usually require my students to write out the content of the chart daily for the first week, and at least once a week thereafter.

Also, Appendix C and Appendix D have all the memory verses and reference charts for the year. Having a copy of these posted in a visible spot such as a bulletin board will encourage frequent review and memorization.

Appendix G: Workbook Answer Key

Lesson 1.1

Lesson 1.2

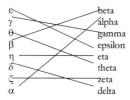

Lesson 1.3

ρ **R**   δ **D**   π **P**   ε **E**
λ **L**   γ **G**   μ **M**   ν **N**

Which two letters work together to make the English /*ing*/ sound? __γγ__
Which Greek letter makes the English /*th*/ sound?
_____θ_____

Lesson 1.5

1.G   2.D   3.A   4.F
5.C   6.B   7.H   8.E

Lesson 2.1

This form of sigma is used at the beginning or middle of a word: ____σ____

We use this form at the end of a word: ___ς___.

Lesson 2.3

A rough breathing mark looks like this: __'__.
When we see it over an initial vowel, we say it like our letter: ____H____.
A smooth breathing mark looks like this: __'__.

Lesson 2.4

1.C   2.E   3.A   4.B   5.D

Lesson 2.5

Learning Greek is fun and not too hard!
So let's get started!

Lesson 3.2

beta β   gamma γ   upsilon υ
iota ι   xi ξ   alpha α
theta θ   rho ρ   lambda λ

Lesson 3.4

λύω   I loose or destroy
πιστεύω   I believe
βλέπω   I see
ἀκούω   I hear
ἔχω   I have or hold

Lesson 3.5

α β γ δ ε ζ η θ ι κ λ μ
ν ξ ο π ρ σ τ υ φ χ ψ ω

Lesson 4.2

—ω	I		—ομεν	we
—εις	you (s)		—ετε	you
—ει	he, she, it		—ουσι	they

Lesson 4.3

βλέπω	I see		βλέπομεν	we see
βλέπεις	you see		βλέπετε	you see
βλέπει	he sees		βλέπουσι	they see

Lesson 4.4

ἀκούω	I hear	ἀκούομεν	we hear
ἀκούεις	you hear	ἀκούετε	you hear
ἀκούει	he hears	ἀκούουσι	they hear

ἔχω	I have	ἔχομεν	we have
ἔχεις	you have	ἔχετε	you have
ἔχει	he has	ἔχουσι	they have

λύω	I loose	λύομεν	we loose
λύεις	you loose	λύετε	you loose
λύει	he looses	λύουσι	they loose

πιστεύω	I believe	πιστεύομεν	we believe
πιστεύεις	you believe	πιστεύετε	you believe
πιστεύει	he believes	πιστεύουσι	they believe

Lesson 4.5

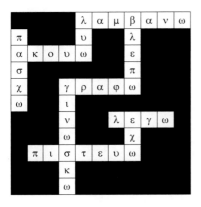

Lesson 5.2

διδάσκω	I teach	διδάσκομεν	we teach
διδάσκεις	you teach	διδάσκετε	you teach
διδάσκει	he teaches	διδάσκουσι	they teach

βάλλω	I throw	βάλλομεν	we throw
βάλλεις	you throw	βάλλετε	you throw
βάλλει	he throws	βάλλουσι	they throw

Lesson 5.3

βλέπεις	you (s) see
ἔχει	he has
λύει	he looses
διδάσκομεν	we teach
ἀκούουσι	they hear
πιστεύετε	you (p) believe
πιστεύει	he believes
βάλλεις	you (s) throw
διδάσκετε	you (p) teach
ἔχουσι	they have

Lesson 5.4

we see	βλέπομεν
they loose	λύουσι
he looses	λύει
we have	ἔχομεν
they teach	διδάσκουσι
I believe	πιστεύω
he throws	βάλλει
you (plural) hear	ἀκούετε
you (singular) hear	ἀκούεις
we teach	διδάσκομεν

Lesson 5.5

γράφω	I write
ὁ λόγος	the word
δέκα	ten
ἔχω	I have or hold
λαμβάνω	I take
ὁ ἄγγελος	the messenger, angel
πιστεύω	I believe
λέγω	I say or speak

Lesson 6.2

εἰμί	I am	ἐσμέν	we are
εἶ	you (s) are	ἐστέ	you are
ἐστί	he is	εἰσί	they are

λύω	λύομεν
λύεις	λύετε
λύει	λύουσι

Lesson 6.3

βλέπω	I see
ἔχεις	you (s) have
ἀκούομεν	we hear
πιστεύουσι	they believe
γινώσκεις	you (s) know
γράφει	he writes
βλέπετε	you (p) see
λαμβάνομεν	we take
λέγουσι	they say
πάσχετε	you (p) suffer

Lesson 6.4

we write	γράφομεν
you (s) say	λέγεις
they take	λαμβάνουσι
he sees	βλέπει
I suffer	πάσχω
you (p) know	γινώσκετε
she believes	πιστεύει
they hear	ἀκούουσι
you (s) have	ἔχεις
we loose	λύομεν

εἰμί	I am		ἐσμέν	we are
εἶ	you (s) are		ἐστέ	you are
ἐστί	he is		εἰσί	they are

Lesson 6.5

```
O  I  D  E  B  S  J  O  B  X  I  D  R  E  M  S  P
E  A  V  M  A  M  R  F  E  A  G  E  A  G  Y  L  R
L  P  T  A  K  E  S  W  L  O  O  S  E  D  C  A  W
N  U  E  N  K  L  H  Q  I  L  R  T  A  S  X  V  O
R  D  A  P  O  S  T  L  E  S  B  R  O  T  H  E  R
E  M  C  R  I  E  L  N  V  A  L  O  H  H  D  A  L
P  S  H  A  V  E  B  P  E  R  U  Y  P  R  O  R  D
U  B  M  N  R  A  S  U  F  F  E  R  T  O  F  E  C
L  H  L  G  O  D  I  R  S  P  Q  R  E  W  O  R  D
I  E  H  E  I  C  D  M  E  S  S  E  N  G  E  R  M
F  I  E  L  D  T  H  U  W  A  P  D  R  A  D  O  N
E  P  A  T  M  F  O  S  P  Y  E  B  U  L  I  S  D
B  W  R  I  T  E  L  A  L  S  A  Y  J  A  N  D  A
R  W  A  S  K  N  D  N  B  R  K  N  O  W  O  N  K
```

Lesson 7.2

ἔχω	ἔχομεν
ἔχεις	ἔχετε
ἔχει	ἔχουσι

Lesson 7.3

ἄνθρωπ<u>ος</u>	ἄνθρωπ<u>οι</u>
ἀνθρώπ<u>ου</u>	ἀνθρώπ<u>ων</u>
ἀνθρώπ<u>ῳ</u>	ἀνθρώπ<u>οις</u>
ἄνθρωπ<u>ον</u>	ἀνθρώπ<u>ους</u>

Writing out all the forms of a noun like this is
called <u>declining</u> the noun.
A group of nouns which follow the same pattern of
endings is called a <u>declension</u>.

Lesson 7.4

ἄνθρωπ<u>ος</u>	ἄνθρωπ<u>οι</u>
ἀνθρώπ<u>ου</u>	ἀνθρώπ<u>ων</u>
ἀνθρώπ<u>ῳ</u>	ἀνθρώπ<u>οις</u>
ἄνθρωπ<u>ον</u>	ἀνθρώπ<u>ους</u>

Lesson 7.5

ὁ ἄγγελος	the messenger, angel
ὁ δοῦλος	the slave
διδάσκω	I teach
καί	and
γινώσκω	I know
ἔχω	I have or hold
ὁ κόσμος	the world
ὁ νόμος	the law
ὁ ἄνθρωπος	the man
ὁ βίος	the life

Lesson 8.1

All of these words are <u>nouns</u>.

Lesson 8.2

λύω	λύομεν
λύεις	λύετε
λύει	λύουσι

Writing a noun with all its different endings is
called <u>declining</u> the noun. A group of nouns which
follows the same pattern is called a <u>declension</u>.

Lesson 8.3

ἀπόστολ<u>ος</u>	ἀπόστολ<u>οι</u>
ἀποστόλ<u>ου</u>	ἀποστόλ<u>ων</u>
ἀποστόλ<u>ῳ</u>	ἀποστόλ<u>οις</u>
ἀπόστολ<u>ον</u>	ἀποστόλ<u>ους</u>

λόγ<u>ος</u>	λόγ<u>οι</u>
λόγ<u>ου</u>	λόγ<u>ων</u>
λόγ<u>ῳ</u>	λόγ<u>οις</u>
λόγ<u>ον</u>	λόγ<u>ους</u>

Lesson 8.4

εἰμί	I am		ἐσμέν	we are
εἶ	you (s) are		ἐστέ	you are
ἐστί	he is		εἰσί	they are

λύει	he looses
βλέπουσι	they see
γινώσκετε	you (p) know
ἔχομεν	we have
γράφω	I write
λαμβάνεις	you (s) take

we see	βλέπομεν
I take	λαμβάνω
they say	λέγουσι
you (s) know	γινώσκεις
you (p) write	γράφετε
I throw	βάλλω

Lesson 9.1

The nouns in today's lesson all end in <u>−ος</u>.
The verbs in today's lesson all end in <u>ω</u>.

Lesson 9.2

γράφω	γράφομεν
γράφεις	γράφετε
γράφει	γράφουσι

We show that a noun is the subject of a sentence by
putting it in the <u>nominative</u> case.
This case is always found on the <u>1st</u> line of the
declension.

Lesson 9.3

We use the <u>nominative</u> case for the subject.

S   V
A slave believes.
δοῦλος πιστεύει.

S   V
A man speaks.
ἄνθρωπος λέγει.

S   V
An apostle knows.
ἀπόστολος γινώσκει.

S   V
A word teaches.
λόγος διδάσκει.

Lesson 9.4

εἰμί	ἐσμέν
εἶ	ἐστέ
ἐστί	εἰσί

S   V
Slaves believe.
δοῦλοι πιστεύουσιν.

S   V
Men speak.
ἄνθρωποι λέγουσιν.

S   V
Apostles know.
ἀπόστολοι γινώσκουσιν.

S   V
Words teach.
λόγοι διδάσκουσιν.

Lesson 9.5

ἔχω	I have or hold
διδάσκω	I teach
ὁ δοῦλος	the slave
ἐγείρω	I raise up
ὁ θάνατος	the death
λαμβάνω	I take
ὁ ἀγρός	the field
ὁ τόπος	the place
ὁ κόσμος	the world
ὁ υἱός	the son

Lesson 10.2

ἐγείρω	I raise up	ἐγείρομεν	we raise up
ἐγείρεις	you raise up	ἐγείρετε	you raise up
ἐγείρει	he raises up	ἐγείρουσι	they raise up

μένω	I remain	μένομεν	we remain
μένεις	you remain	μένετε	you remain
μένει	he remains	μένουσι	they remain

teachers	διδάσκαλοι
a brother	ἀδελφός
heavens	οὐρανοί
places	τόποι
an apostle	ἀπόστολος
words	λόγοι
worlds	κόσμοι
a man	ἄνθρωπος
God	θεός
a lord	κύριος
fields	ἀγροί
slaves	δοῦλοι

Lesson 10.3

S   V
A law remains.
νόμος μένει.

S   V
Teachers judge.
διδάσκαλοι κρίνουσιν.

S   V
You (s) throw.
βάλλεις.

S   V
A lord leads.
κύριος ἄγει.

S   V
We hear.
ἀκούομεν.

Lesson 10.4

εἰμί	ἐσμέν
εἶ	ἐστέ
ἐστί	εἰσί

διδάσκετε.
You (p) teach.

ἀπόστολοι βλέπουσι.
Apostles see.

υἱὸς ἄγει.
A son leads.

ἔχεις.
You (s) have/hold.

οἶκος μένει.
A house remains.

Lesson 10.5

ὁ βίος	N	the live
ὁ κύριος	N	the son
ἔχω	V	I have or hold
ὁ τόπος	N	the place
λύω	V	I loose or destroy
πέμπω	V	I send
ὁ λίθος	N	the stone
ἄγω	V	I lead
φέρω	V	I bear, bring
ὁ νόμος	N	the law
πάσχω	V	I suffer

Lesson 11.1

The prefix εὐ means good. *Eulology* comes from the prefix εὐ and the Greek word λογος. When someone delivers a eulogy, they say good words.

Lesson 11.2

ἄγω	ἄγομεν	γινώσκω	γινώσκομεν
ἄγεις	ἄγετε	γινώσκεις	γινώσκετε
ἄγει	ἄγουσι	γινώσκει	γινώσκουσι

Greek nouns are masculine, feminine, or neuter. 2nd declension nouns that end in −ος are masculine and nouns that end in −ον are neuter.

Lesson 11.3

ἄνθρωπος	ἄνθρωποι
ἀνθρώπου	ἀνθρώπων
ἀνθρώπῳ	ἀνθρώποις
ἄνθρωπον	ἀνθρώπους

δῶρον	δῶρα
δώρου	δώρων
δώρῳ	δώροις
δῶρον	δῶρα

Lesson 11.4

εἰμί	ἐσμέν
εἶ	ἐστέ
ἐστί	εἰσί

τέκνον	τέκνα
τέκνου	τέκνων
τέκνῳ	τέκνοις
τέκνον	τέκνα

εὐαγγέλιον	εὐαγγέλια
εὐαγγελίου	εὐαγγελίων
εὐαγγελίῳ	εὐαγγελίοις
εὐαγγέλιον	εὐαγγέλια

πρόσωπον	πρόσωπα
προσώπου	προσώπων
προσώπῳ	προσώποις
πρόσωπον	πρόσωπα

ἱερόν	ἱερά
ἱεροῦ	ἱερῶν
ἱερῷ	ἱεροῖς
ἱερόν	ἱερά

Lesson 12.1

The new vocabulary words this week belong to the 2nd declension.
The first four are neuter. The last word in our list is masculine.

Lesson 12.2

πέμπω	πέμπομεν
πέμπεις	πέμπετε
πέμπει	πέμπουσι
πιστεύω	πιστεύομεν
πιστεύεις	πιστεύετε
πιστεύει	πιστεύουσι

	gender	number	translation
οὐρανοί	M	P	heavens
τόπος	M	S	place
τέκνα	N	P	children
εὐαγγέλια	N	P	gospels
βιβλίον	N	S	book
διδάσκαλοι	M	P	teachers
δοῦλοι	M	P	slaves
θεός	M	S	God
πλοῖον	N	S	boat
ἱερά	N	P	temples

Lesson 12.3

S   V
Books remain.
βιβλία μένουσιν.

S   V
A boat leads.
πλοῖον ἄγει.

S   V
A gospel teaches.
εὐαγγέλιον διδάσκει.

S   V
Sinners suffer.
ἀμαρτολοὶ πάσχουσιν.

Lesson 12.4

εἰμί	ἐσμέν
εἶ	ἐστέ
ἐστί	εἰσί

ἱερόν μένει.	A temple remains.
δαιμόνιον πάσχει.	A demon suffers.
ἁμαρτωλὸς ἀκούει.	A sinner hears.
δῶρα διδάσκουσιν.	Gifts teach.
βιβλίον ἄγει.	A book leads.

Lesson 12.5

Lesson 13.1

ἄρτος and τυφλός are from the 2nd declension.
They are both masculine nouns.

Lesson 13.2

σώζω	σώζομεν	βαίνω	βαίνομεν
σώζεις	σώζετε	βαίνεις	βαίνετε
σώζει	σώζουσι	βαίνει	βαίνουσι

Today we've talked about linking verbs. Linking
verbs connect one side of the sentence with the
other. Nouns that come after a linking verb take
the nominative case.

Lesson 13.3

ἄνθρωπος	ἄνθρωποι
ἀνθρώπου	ἀνθρώπων
ἀνθρώπῳ	ἀνθρώποις
ἄνθρωπον	ἀνθρώπους

δῶρον	δῶρα
δώρου	δώρων
δώρῳ	δώροις
δῶρον	δῶρα

S   LV PN
God is lord.
θεός ἐστι κύριος.

S   LV PN
You are a child.
εἶ τέκνον.

S   LV PN
Apostles are teachers.
ἀπόστολοί εἰσι διδάσκαλοι.

S   LV PN
We are sinners.
ἐσμὲν ἁμαρτολοί.

Lesson 13.4

εἰμί	ἐσμέν
εἶ	ἐστέ
ἐστί	εἰσί

θεός ἐστι διδάσκαλος.
God is a teacher.

ἐσμὲν υἱοί.
We are sons.

ἱερόν ἐστι τόπος.
A temple is a place.

ἐστὶ τυφλός.
He is a blind man.

ἀδελφοί εἰσι δοῦλοι.
Brothers are servants.

Lesson 13.5

ἄγω	I lead
φέρω	I bear, bring
σώζω	I save
λέγω	I say or speak
μένω	I remain
βάλλω	I throw
βλέπω	I see
ἐγείρω	I raise up
γράφω	I write
βαίνω	I go

All of these words are verbs.
The −ω ending represents the pronoun I.

Lesson 14.1

ἀκούω	I hear
δέκα	ten
πάσχω	I suffer
ὁ λίθος	the stone
ὁ οὐρανός	the heaven
ὁ βιός	the life

ὁ ἄγγελος	the angel
ὁ κόσμος	the lord
μένω	I remain
πέμπω	I send

Lesson 14.2

πέμπω	πέμπομεν
πέμπεις	πέμπετε
πέμπει	πέμπουσι

πιστεύω	πιστεύομεν
πιστεύεις	πιστεύετε
πιστεύει	πιστεύουσι

Susie's bike got all wet in the rain.
The sun goes down at the end of the day.
I wanted to play my brother's game.
The edge of the plate is chipped.

Lesson 14.3

ἄνθρωπος	ἄνθρωποι
ἀνθρώπου	ἀνθρώπων
ἀνθρώπῳ	ἀνθρώποις
ἄνθρωπον	ἀνθρώπους

δῶρον	δῶρα
δώρου	δώρων
δώρῳ	δώροις
δῶρον	δῶρα

τόπος	place
υἱοῦ	of the son
λόγου	of the word
οἴκων	of the houses
ἀδελφῶν	of the brothers
δοῦλοι	servants
νόμος	law
ἀποστόλου	of the apostle

Lesson 14.4

εἰμί	ἐσμέν
εἶ	ἐστέ
ἐστί	εἰσί

εὐαγγέλιον κυρίου διδάσκει.
A gospel of a lord teaches.

ἀνθρώπου υἱοὶ γράφουσιν.
Sons of a man write.

διδάσκαλος δούλων κρίνει.
A teacher of servants judges.

τέκνον θεοῦ λέγει.
A child of God speaks.

ἀπόστολος θεοῦ μένει.
An apostle of God remains.

Lesson 15.1

ὁ τόπος	place
ἐγείρω	I raise up
πιστεύω	I believe
ὁ ἀγρός	field
λαμβάνω	I take
ὁ τυφλός	blind man
τό πλοῖον	boat
ὁ ἄρτος	bread
τό πρόσωπον	face
κρίνω	I judge

Lesson 15.2

βαπτίζω	βαπτίζομεν		φέρω	φέρομεν
βαπτίζεις	βαπτίζετε		φέρεις	φέρετε
βαπτίζει	βαπτίζουσι		φέρει	φέρουσι

νόμος	M	S	Nom.	law
ἀγγέλων	M	P	Gen.	of angels
βίοι	M	P	Nom.	lives
λόγου	M	S	Gen.	of a word
θεοῦ	M	S	Gen.	of God
ἀδελφοῦ	M	S	Gen.	of brothers
ἀγρῶν	M	P	Gen.	of fields
ἄνθρωποι	M	P	Nom.	men
ἀπόστολοι	M	P	Nom.	apostles
δούλων	M	P	Gen.	of servants

Lesson 15.3

ἄνθρωπος	ἄνθρωποι
ἀνθρώπου	ἀνθρώπων
ἀνθρώπῳ	ἀνθρώποις
ἄνθρωπον	ἀνθρώπους

δῶρον	δῶρα
δώρου	δώρων
δώρῳ	δώροις
δῶρον	δῶρα

stones	λίθοι
place	τόπος
of a slave	δούλου
of a face	προσώπου
of angels	ἀγγέλων
gifts	δῶρα

Lesson 15.4

εἰμί	ἐσμέν
εἶ	ἐστέ
ἐστί	εἰσί

The subject must be in the <u>nominative</u> case.
Possessives take the <u>genitive</u> case.

  S   V
They believe.
πιστεύουσιν.

  S   poss   V
A book <u>of a son</u> teaches.
βιβλίον υἱοῦ διδάσκει.

  S   poss   V
Slaves <u>of a man</u> hear.
δοῦλοι ἀνθρώπου ἀκούουσιν.

  S   V
Brothers write.
ἀδελφοὶ γράφουσιν.

Lesson 16.1

Today's vocabulary words are <u>nouns</u>. Nouns that end in −α are part of the <u>first</u> declension.

Lesson 16.2

ἐγείρω	ἐγείρομεν		μένω	μένομεν
ἐγείρεις	ἐγείρετε		μένεις	μένετε
ἐγείρει	ἐγείρουσι		μένει	μένουσι

Masculine nouns usually end in <u>−ος</u>, neuter nouns in <u>−ον</u>, and feminine nouns usually in <u>−α or η</u>.

Lesson 16.3

ἄνθρωπος	ἄνθρωποι
ἀνθρώπου	ἀνθρώπων
ἀνθρώπῳ	ἀνθρώποις
ἄνθρωπον	ἀνθρώπους

δῶρον	δῶρα
δώρου	δώρων
δώρῳ	δώροις
δῶρον	δῶρα

ἀλήθεια	nominative	ἀλήθειαι
ἀληθείας	genitive	ἀλήθειων
ἀληθείᾳ	dative	ἀληθείαις
ἀλήθειαν	accusative	ἀληθείας

Lesson 16.4

εἰμί	ἐσμέν
εἶ	ἐστέ
ἐστί	εἰσί

  S   V
A kingdom hears.
βασιλεία ἀκούει.

  S   V
Churches lead.
ἐκκλησίαι ἄγουσιν.

  S   V
Truth teaches.
ἀλήθεια διδάσκει.

  S   V
Days remain.
ἡμέραι μένουσιν.

  S   V
A church believes.
ἐκκλησία πιστεύει.

Lesson 16.5

τέκνα	N	P	Nom.	children
ἐκκλησία	F	S	Nom.	church
τυφλοῦ	M	S	Gen.	of the blind man
βίοι	M	P	Nom.	lives
ὧραι	F	P	Nom.	hours
ἱερῶν	N	P	Gen.	of the temples
ἡμέρα	F	S	Nom.	day

Lesson 17.2

ἄγω	ἄγομεν		γινώσκω	γινώσκομεν
ἄγεις	ἄγετε		γινώσκεις	γινώσκετε
ἄγει	ἄγουσι		γινώσκει	γινώσκουσι

Nouns that end in <u>−η</u> belong to the <u>1ˢᵗ</u> declension. Nouns that end in <u>−α</u> or <u>−η</u> are <u>feminine</u>.

Lesson 17.3

γραφή	nom	γραφαί
γραφῆς	gen	γραφῶν
γραφῇ	dat	γραφαῖς
γραφήν	acc	γραφάς

ἀλήθεια	ἀλήθειαι
ἀληθείας	ἀλήθειων
ἀληθείᾳ	ἀληθείαις
ἀλήθειαν	ἀληθείας

Lesson 17.4

  S   V
Commandments teach.
ἐντολαὶ διδάσκουσιν.

    S   V
A kingdom hears.
βασιλεία ἀκούει.

    S   V
A parable teaches.
παραβολὴ διδάσκει.

N   V
εἰρήνη μένει.
A peace remains.

N   V
ἐκκλησίαι ἀκούουσιν.
Churches hear.

N   V
γραφὴ κρίνει.
Scripture judges.

Lesson 18.1

These nouns belong to the 1st declension.
They are all <u>feminine</u>.

Lesson 18.2

πέμπω	πέμπομεν	βαπτίζω	βαπτίζομεν
πέμπεις	πέμπετε	βαπτίζεις	βαπτίζετε
πέμπει	πέμπουσι	βαπτίζει	βαπτίζουσι

of a commandment	ἐντολῆς
of a sin	ἁμαρτίας
of a voice	φωνῆς
of parables	παραβολῶν
of a church	ἐκκλησίας
of hearts	καρδιῶν
of kingdoms	βασιλειῶν
of love	ἀγάπης
of peace	εἰρήνης
of truth	ἀληθείας

Lesson 18.3

δῶρον	δῶρα
δώρου	Δώρων
δώρῳ	δώροις
δῶρον	δῶρα

ἀλήθεια	ἀλήθειαι
ἀληθείας	ἀληθειῶν
ἀληθείᾳ	ἀληθείαις
ἀλήθειαν	ἀληθείας

ἀλήθειαι	of truths
ἡμέρας	of a day
ζωή	life
ζωαί	lives
ψυχῶν	of souls
ἁμαρτίας	of sin
ἐντολαί	commandments
καρδιῶν	of hearts
ὥρα	hour
εἰρήνης	of a peace

Lesson 18.4

N   V
φωνὴ λέγει.
A voice speaks.

N   V
ὥρα μένει.
An hour remains.

N   V
ἀπόστολος βαπτίζει.
An apostle baptizes.

N   V
παραβολαὶ διδάσκουσιν.
Parables teach.

N   V
καρδιαὶ κρίνουσιν.
Hearts judge.

Lesson 18.5

ἡ ἀλήθεια	the	truth
ἡ ἐκκλησία	the	church
ἡ ὥρα	the	hour
ἡ παραβολή	the	parable
ἡ ἐντολη	the	commandment
ἡ καρδία	the	heart
ἡ ἁμαρτία	the	sin
ἡ βασιλεία	the	kingdom
ἡ ἡμέρα	the	day
ἡ γραφή	the	writing, scripture
ἡ εἰρήνη	the	peace
ἡ ζωή	the	life
ἡ ψυχή	the	soul, life
ἡ ἀγάπη	the	love

Lesson 19.2

θέλω	θέλομεν
θέλεις	θέλετε
θέλει	θέλουσι

ἁμαρτάνω	ἁμαρτάνομεν
ἁμαρτάνεις	ἁμαρτάνετε
ἁμαρτάνει	ἁμαρτάνουσι

Nominative:	*Singular*		*Plural*
1st dec. Feminine:	−α −η		−αι
2nd dec., Masculine:	−ος		−οι
2nd dec., Neuter:	−ον		−α

Genitive:	*Singular*		*Plural*
1st dec. Feminine:	−ας −ης		−ων
2nd dec., Masculine:	−ου		−ων
2nd dec., Neuter:	−ου		−ων

ἐπαγγελιῶν	N	P	Gen.	of the promises
τυφλοί	M	P	Nom.	blind men

φωνή	F	S	Nom.	voice
εὐαγγελίου	N	S	Gen.	of the gospel
ἀγάπαι	F	P	Nom.	loves

Lesson 19.3

ἄνθρωπος	ἄνθρωποι
ἀνθρώπου	ἀνθρώπων
ἀνθρώπῳ	ἀνθρώποις
ἄνθρωπον	ἀνθρώπους

ἀλήθεια	ἀλήθειαι
ἀληθείας	ἀληθειῶν
ἀληθείᾳ	ἀληθείαις
ἀλήθειαν	ἀληθείας

N   V
ἀπόστολος βαπτίζει.
An apostle baptizes.

N   G   V
ἀπόστολος ἐκκλησίας διδάσκει.
An apostle of a church teaches.

N   G   V
φωνὴ ἀληθείας σώζει.
A voice of truth saves.

N   G   V
διδάσκαλοι ἐντολῶν κρίνουσιν.
Teachers of commandments judge.

N   G   V
δοῦλοι ἁμαρτολῶν πάσχουσιν.
Servants of sinners suffer.

Lesson 19.4

S   V
A voice speaks.
φωνὴ λέγει.

S   poss   V
A voice of God speaks.
φωνὴ θεοῦ λέγει.

S   poss   V
An hour of a day remains.
ὥρα ἡμέρας μένει.

S   V
Boats go.
πλοῖα βαίνουσιν.

S   poss   V
Boats of apostles go.
πλοῖα ἀποστόλων βαίνουσιν.

Lesson 20.1

ὁ διδάσκαλος	the teacher
ἡ ἐπαγγελία	the promise
τό εὐαγγέλιον	the gospel
κρίνω	I judge
τό πρόσωπον	the face
ἡ χαρά	the joy
διδάσκω	I teach
τό δῶρον	the gift
ἡ εἰρήνη	the peace

Lesson 20.2

κρίνω	κρίνομεν
κρίνεις	κρίνετε
κρίνει	κρίνουσι

διδάσκω	διδάσκομεν
διδάσκεις	διδάσκετε
διδάσκει	διδάσκουσι

ὁ ἄγγελος	τό τέκνον
τό τόπος	ἡ ψυχή
ἡ ἀλήθεια	ὁ λόγος
ἡ ἐκκλησία	ἡ ζωή

Lesson 20.3

δῶρον	δῶρα
δώρου	δώρων
δώρῳ	δώροις
δῶρον	δῶρα

ἀλήθεια	ἀλήθειαι
ἀληθείας	ἀληθειῶν
ἀληθείᾳ	ἀληθείαις
ἀλήθειαν	ἀληθείας

The man teaches.
ὁ ἄνθρωπος διδάσκει.

ἡ εἰρήνη βασιλείας μένει.
The peace of a kingdom remains.

Lesson 20.4

εἰμί	ἐσμέν
εἶ	ἐστέ
ἐστί	εἰσί

Subjects must be in the nominative case in Greek.
Possessives must be in the genitive case in Greek.

S   poss.   V
ὁ ἄγγελος θεοῦ βλέπει.
The angel of God sees.

    S   V
τὸ εὐαγγέλιον διδάσκει.
The gospel teaches.

    S V
The child hears.
τὸ τέκνον ἀκούει.

    S V
The lord judges.
ὁ κύριος κρίνει.

    poss S V
A slave's brother baptizes.
ἀδελφὸς δούλου βαπτίζει.

Lesson 21.1

ἡ οἰκία	feminine
ὁ καρπός	masculine
ὁ Χριστός	masculine

Lesson 21.2

θέλω	θέλομεν		φέρω	φέρομεν
θέλεις	θέλετε		φέρεις	φέρετε
θέλει	θέλουσι		φέρει	φέρουσι

Lesson 21.3

ἄνθρωπος	ἄνθρωποι
ἀνθρώπου	ἀνθρώπων
ἀνθρώπῳ	ἀνθρώποις
ἄνθρωπον	ἀνθρώπους

ἀλήθεια	ἀλήθειαι
ἀληθείας	ἀληθειῶν
ἀληθείᾳ	ἀληθείαις
ἀλήθειαν	ἀληθείας

	gender	number	case
τοῦ	M or N	S	Gen
ὁ	M	S	Nom
τῆς	F	S	Gen
αἱ	F	P	Nom
τῶν	M, F, or N	P	Gen
τά	N	P	Nom

Lesson 21.4

τῆς ἀληθείας	F	S	Gen
of the truth			
τῶν ὡρῶν	F	P	Gen
of the hours			
οἱ ἄνθρωποι	M	P	Nom
the men			

ὁ υἱός	M	S	Nom
the son			
τό δῶρον	N	S	Nom
the gift			

Lesson 22.2

σώζω	σώζομεν		εἰμί	ἐσμέν
σώζεις	σώζετε		εἶ	ἐστέ
σώζει	σώζουσι		ἐστί	εἰσί

Lesson 22.3

		Singular	
	masc.	*fem.*	*neut.*
Nom.	ἀγαθός	ἀγαθή	ἀγαθόν
Gen.	ἀγαθοῦ	ἀγαθῆς	ἀγαθοῦ

		Plural	
	masc.	*fem.*	*neut.*
Nom.	ἀγαθοί	ἀγαθαί	ἀγαθά
Gen.	ἀγαθῶν	ἀγαθῶν	ἀγαθῶν

In this chart, the endings for the singular masculine and the singular neuter differ from the same forms of 'the' (ὁ τό). However, all other endings are the same.

Lesson 22.4

		gender	no.	case
ἡ	——η ζωή	F	S	Nom
τῶν	——ων ἀδέλφων	M	P	Gen
οἱ	——οι κόσμοι	M	P	Nom
τῆς	——ης ἡμέρας	F	S	Gen
τοῦ	——ου λόγου	M	S	Gen

(Any of this week's vocabulary words can be used to fill in the blanks, but the endings ought to be as noted.)

Lesson 23.2

πιστεύω	πιστεύομεν
πιστεύεις	πιστεύετε
πιστεύει	πιστεύουσι

καλύπτω	καλύπτομεν
καλύπτεις	καλύπτετε
καλύπτει	καλύπτουσι

Lesson 23.3

    S   *V*
The servant speaks.
ὁ δοῦλος λέγει.

    adj S   *V*
The faithful servant speaks.
ὁ πιστὸς δοῦλος λέγει.

adj   S   poss   V
The faithful servant <u>of the man</u> speaks.
ὁ πιστὸς δοῦλος τοῦ ἀνθρώπου λέγει.

S   poss   V
The brother <u>of the man</u> teaches.
ὁ ἀδελφὸς τοῦ ἀνθρώπου διδάσκει.

adj   S   poss   V
The good brother <u>of the man</u> teaches.
ὁ ἀγαθὸς ἀδελφὸς τοῦ ἀνθρώπου διδάσκει.
(or καλὸς may be used instead of ἀγαθὸς)

Lesson 23.4

N (nom)   V
ὁ ἀπόστολος γράφει.
The apostle writes.

N (nom)   N (gen)   V
ὁ ἀπόστολος τοῦ κυρίου γράφει.
The apostle of the Lord writes.

adj(nom)   N(nom)   N(gen)   V
ὁ πιστὸς ἀπόστολος τοῦ κυρίου γράφει.
The faithful apostle of the Lord writes.

adj-nom   N(nom)   adj-gen   N(gen)
ὁ πιστὸς ἀπόστολος τοῦ ἀγαθοῦ κυρίου
V
γράφει.
The faithful apostle of the good Lord writes.

Lesson 23.5

	Singular		
Nom.	πιστός	πιστή	πιστόν
Gen.	πιστοῦ	πιστῆς	πιστοῦ
	Plural		
Nom.	πιστοί	πισταί	πιστά
Gen.	πιστῶν	πιστῶν	πιστῶν

	Singular		
Nom.	πρῶτος	πρώτη	πρῶτον
Gen.	πρώτου	πρώτης	πρώτου
	Plural		
Nom.	πρῶτοι	πρῶται	πρῶτα
Gen.	πρώτων	πρώτων	πρώτων

	Singular		
Nom.	ἅγιος	ἅγια	ἅγιον
Gen.	ἁγίου	ἁγίας	ἁγίου
	Plural		
Nom.	ἅγιοι	ἅγιαι	ἅγια
Gen.	ἁγίων	ἁγίων	ἁγίων

	Singular		
Nom.	πονηρός	πονηρά	πονηρόν
Gen.	πονηροῦ	πονηρᾶς	πονηροῦ

	Plural		
Nom.	πονηροί	πονηραί	πονηρά
Gen.	πονηρῶν	πονηρῶν	πονηρῶν

Lesson 24.2

ἀποστέλλω	ἀποστέλλομεν
ἀποστέλλεις	ἀποστέλλετε
ἀποστέλλει	ἀποστέλλουσι

λύω	λύομεν
λύεις	λύετε
λύει	λύουσι

	gender	no.	case
τῆς <u>ἀγαθῆς</u> ζωῆς	F	S	Gen.
τό <u>πονηρὸν</u> δαιμόνιον	N	S	Nom.
τά <u>μικρὰ</u> πλοῖα	N	P	Nom.
ὁ <u>δεύτερος</u> τυφλός	M	S	Nom.
τῶν <u>πιστῶν</u> ἔργων	N	P	Gen.

Lesson 24.3

S   V
The blind man hears.
ὁ τυφλὸς ἀκούει.

adj   S   V
The faithful blind man hears.
ὁ πιστὸς τυφλὸς ἀκούει.

adj   S   poss   V
The faithful blind man <u>of the kingdom</u> hears.
ὁ πιστὸς τυφλὸς τῆς βασιλείης ἀκούει.

S   V
A blind man hears.
τυφλὸς ἀκούει.
(Remember that in Greek there is no word for 'a'.)

adj   S   poss   V
The other servant <u>of the man</u> speaks.
(or, The man's other servant speaks.)
ὁ ἄλλος δοῦλος τοῦ ἀνθρώπου λέγει.

Lesson 24.4

N(nom)   V
ἡ χαρὰ μένει.
The joy remains.

N(nom)   N(gen)   V
ἡ χαρὰ ἀνθρώπου μένει.
The joy of man remains.

N(nom)   adj(gen)   N(gen)   V
ἡ χαρὰ τοῦ ἀγαθοῦ ἀνθρώπου μένει.
The joy of the good man remains.

	adj(nom)	N(nom)	adj(gen)	N(gen)

ἡ πρώπη χαρὰ τοῦ ἀγαθοῦ ἀνθρώπου
          ∨
μένει.
The first joy of the good man remains.

	adj(gen)	N(gen)	adj(nom)	N(nom)

τοῦ ἀγαθοῦ ἀνθρώπου ἡ πρώπη χαρὰ
          ∨
μένει.
The first joy of the good man remains.

Lesson 25.1

ἐκ changes its form to ἐξ when the next word begins with a <u>vowel</u>.

Lesson 25.2

πιστεύω	πιστεύομεν
πιστεύεις	πιστεύετε
πιστεύει	πιστεύουσι

εἰμί	ἐσμέν
εἶ	ἐστέ
ἐστί	εἰσί

Lesson 25.3

ἄνθρωπος	ἄνθρωποι
ἀνθρώπου	ἀνθρώπων
ἀνθρώπῳ	ἀνθρώποις
ἄνθρωπον	ἀνθρώπους

δῶρον	δῶρα
δώρου	δώρων
δώρῳ	δώροις
δῶρον	δῶρα

ἀλήθεια	ἀλήθειαι
ἀληθείας	ἀληθειῶν
ἀληθείᾳ	ἀληθείαις
ἀλήθειαν	ἀληθείας

from God	ἀπὸ θεοῦ
through the church	διὰ τῆς ἐκκλησίας
out of the kingdom	ἐκ τῆς βασιλείας
out of a field	ἐξ ἀγροῦ
with a slave	μετὰ δούλου

Lesson 25.4

Feminine adjectives use alphas if the last letter of the adjective stem is ι, ε, or ρ.

The law is from God.
ὁ νόμος ἐστί ἀπὸ θεοῦ.

A slave goes out of a field.
δοῦλος βαίνει ἐξ ἀγροῦ.

The child remains with a slave.
τό τέκνον μένει μετὰ δούλου.

Lesson 26.1

		declension	gender
ἡ	ἔρημος	2<u>nd</u>	F
ἡ	ὁδος	2<u>nd</u>	F

Lesson 26.2

singular		plural
ἔρημο<u>ς</u>	Nom	ἔρημο<u>ι</u>
ἔρημο<u>υ</u>	Gen	ἔρημ<u>ων</u>
ἔρημ<u>ῳ</u>	Dat	ἔρημο<u>ις</u>
ἔρημο<u>ν</u>	Acc	ἔρημ<u>ους</u>

singular		plural
ὁδ<u>ός</u>	Nom	ὁδ<u>οί</u>
ὁδ<u>οῦ</u>	Gen	ὁδ<u>ῶν</u>
ὁδ<u>ῷ</u>	Dat	ὁδ<u>οῖς</u>
ὁδ<u>όν</u>	Acc	ὁδ<u>ούς</u>

Lesson 26.3

κατὰ τοῦ <u>νόμου</u>
against the law

παρὰ τοῦ <u>εὐαγγελίου</u>
from the gospel

περὶ τῆς <u>ἐπαγγελίας</u>
about the promise

ἀπὸ τοῦ <u>βιβλίου</u>
from the book

μετὰ τοῦ <u>ἁμαρτωλοῦ</u>
with the sinner

Lesson 26.4

S	V	P	OP

He teaches against the law.
διδάσκει κατὰ τοῦ νόμου.

S	V	P	OP

They teach from the gospel.
διδάσκουσι παρὰ (or ἀπὸ)τοῦ εὐαγγελίου.

S	V	P	OP

I teach about the promise.
διδάσκω περὶ τῆς ἐπαγγελίας.

S	V	P	OP

We teach from the book.
διδάσκομεν ἀπὸ τοῦ βιβλίου.

S	V	P	OP

You (s) go with the child.
βαίνεις μετὰ τοῦ τέκνου.

Lesson 27.1

ὁ κόσμος	the world	noun
ἄγω	I lead	verb
ὁ ἄγγελος	the angel	noun
φέρω	I bear, bring	verb
βάλλω	I throw	verb
ἀπό	from	prep
ὁ τόπος	the place	noun
τό τέκνον	the child	noun
διά	through	prep
ὁ θεός	the god	noun

Lesson 27.2

art N:n/s/n   V
τὸ τέκνον βάλλει.

V   prep   art   N:n/s/g
μένω μετὰ τοῦ τέκνου.

V   prep   art   N:n/p/g
μένουσι μετὰ τῶν τέκνων.

art N:m/p/n   V   prep   art   N:n/p/g
οἱ δοῦλοι μένουσι μετὰ τῶν τέκνων.

Lesson 27.3

ὁ ἄγγελος τοῦ θεοῦ μένει μετὰ τοῦ
ἀνθρώπου.
The angel of God remains with the man.

τὸ τέκνον βάλλει.
The child throws.

μένω μετὰ τοῦ τέκνου.
I remain with the child.

μένουσι μετὰ τῶν τέκνων.
They remain with the children.

οἱ δοῦλοι μένουσι μετὰ τῶν τέκνων.
The servants remain with the children.

Lesson 27.4

The child speaks.
τὸ τέκνον λέγει.

A child leads.
τέκνον ἄγει.

The day is from God.
ἡ ἡμέρα ἐστὶ παρὰ θεοῦ.
(The word ἀπὸ could also be used instead of
παρὰ.)

The beautiful day is from God.
ἡ καλὴ ἡμέρα ἐστὶ παρὰ θεοῦ.

The book is about God.
τὸ βιβλίον ἐστὶ περὶ θεοῦ.

Lesson 28.1

βλέπω	I see	verb
ὁ ἀδελφός	the brother	noun
ἡ ἀλήθεια	the truth	noun
ἀγαθός	good	adjective
ἡ ἀγάπη	the love	noun
ἀκούω	I hear	verb
ὁ ἄρτος	the bread	noun
τό βιβλίον	the book	noun
τό πλοῖον	the boat	noun
περί	about	prep

Lesson 28.2

ἀκούω	ἀκούομεν
ἀκούεις	ἀκούετε
ἀκούει	ἀκούουσι

εἰμί	ἐσμέν
εἶ	ἐστέ
ἐστί	εἰσί

Lesson 28.3

ἄνθρωπος	ἄνθρωποι
ἀνθρώπου	ἀνθρώπων
ἀνθρώπῳ	ἀνθρώποις
ἄνθρωπον	ἀνθρώπους

δῶρον	δῶρα
δώρου	δώρων
δώρῳ	δώροις
δῶρον	δῶρα

ἀλήθεια	ἀλήθειαι
ἀληθείας	ἀληθειῶν
ἀληθείᾳ	ἀληθείαις
ἀλήθειαν	ἀληθείας

N:m/s/n   V
δοῦλος βαίνει.

art   adj:m/s/n   N:m/s/n   V
ὁ   ἀγαθὸς   δοῦλος   βαίνει.

art   N:m/s/n   V   prep   art   N:f/p/g
ὁ   ἀπόστολος   διδάσκει   περὶ   τῶν   ἐντολῶν.

art   adj:m/p/n   N:m/p/n   V   prep
οἱ   κακοὶ   δοῦλοι   ἁμαρτάνουσι   κατὰ
art   N:m/p/g
τῶν   κυρίων.

art n   N:f/s/n   art   N:m/s/g   V
ἡ   γραφὴ   τοῦ   ἀνθρώπου   ἐστὶ
adj:f/s/n   N:f/s/n
πιστὴ   γραφή.

Lesson 28.4

δοῦλος βαίνει.
A slave goes.

ὁ ἀγαθὸς δοῦλος βαίνει.
The good slave goes.

ὁ ἀπόστολος διδάσκει περὶ τῶν ἐντολῶν.
The apostle teaches about the commandments.

οἱ κακοὶ δοῦλοι ἁμαρτάνουσι κατὰ τῶν κυρίων.
The bad slaves sin against the lords.

ἡ γραφὴ τοῦ ἀνθρώπου ἐστὶ πιστὴ γραφή.
The writing of the man is faithful writing.

Lesson 29.1

τό ἔργον	the work	noun
γινώσκω	I know	verb
ὁ ἀπόστολος	the apostle	noun
ἡ βασιλεία	the kingdom	noun
ἄλλος	other	adj
ἄγω	I lead	verb
ἡ ἁμαρτία	the sin	noun
ὁ ἁμαρτωλός	the sinner	noun
κατά	against	prep

Lesson 29.2

γινώσκω	γινώσκομεν
γινώσκεις	γινώσκετε
γινώσκει	γινώσκουσι

ἄγω	ἄγομεν
ἄγεις	ἄγετε
ἄγει	ἄγουσι

S   I´
We go.
βαίνομεν.

S   I´   prep   OP
He teaches from the book.
διδάσκει ἀπὸ τοῦ βιβλίου.

S   I´
They know.
γινώσκουσι.

S   I´   prep   OP
She knows about God.
γινώσκει περὶ θεοῦ.

S   I´
You (p) hear.
ἀκούετε.

Lesson 29.3

art   N:n/s/n   I´
τό δαιμόνιον γινώσκει.

verb
λέγετε.

art   N:n/s/n   I´   prep   art   N:m/s/g
τό δαιμόνιον γινώσκει περὶ τοῦ θεοῦ.

I´
διδάσκουσι.

I´   prep   art   N:m/p/g
γράφετε περὶ τῶν ἁμαρτωλῶν.

Lesson 29.4

τό δαιμόνιον γινώσκει.
The demon knows.

λέγετε.
You (p) speak.

τό δαιμόνιον γινώσκει περὶ τοῦ θεοῦ.
The demon knows about the God.

διδάσκουσι.
They teach.

γράφετε περὶ τῶν ἁμαρτωλῶν.
You write about the sinners.

Lesson 30.1

βαίνω	I go	verb
μετά	with	prep
παρά	from	prep
γράφω	I write	verb
δοῦλος	slave	noun
γραφή	writing, scripture	noun
ἐγείρω	I raise up	verb
ἀπό	from	prep
βαπτίζω	I baptize	verb
σώζω	I save	verb

Lesson 30.2

βαίνω	βαίνομεν
βαίνεις	βαίνετε
βαίνει	βαίνουσι

γράφω	γράφομεν
γράφεις	γράφετε
γράφει	γράφουσι

δοῦλοι	M	P	Nom	slaves
γραφῆς	F	S	Gen	of the writing (or scripture)
ἀληθειῶν	F	P	Gen	of the truths
δῶρον	N	S	Nom	gift

θανάτου M S Gen of the death

Lesson 30.3

<u>ἀγαθοὶ</u> δοῦλοι	M	S	Nom
<u>ἄλλης</u> γραφῆς	F	S	Gen
<u>πρῶται</u> ἀληθείαι	F	P	Nom
<u>καλόν</u> δῶρον	N	S	Nom
<u>ἐσχάτοι</u> θανάτοι	M	P	Nom

Lesson 30.4

The faithful apostles teach about God.
οἱ πιστοὶ ἀπόστολοι διδάσκουσι περὶ θεοῦ.

The first child goes out of the field.
τὸ πρῶτον τέκνον βαίνει ἐκ τοῦ ἀγροῦ.

The faithful apostles teach about the good God.
οἱ πιστοὶ ἀπόστολοι διδάσκουσι περὶ τοῦ
ἀγαθοῦ (or καλοῦ) θεοῦ.

The last child goes through the field.
τὸ ἔσκατον τέκνον βαίνει διὰ τοῦ ἀγροῦ.

The last child goes through the field of the blind
man. (...the blind man's field)
τὸ ἔσκατον τέκνον βαίνει διὰ τοῦ ἀγροῦ
τοῦ τυφλοῦ.

About Christine Gatchell

Christine Gatchell and her husband, Matt, homeschool their five children in Red Lion, Pennsylvania. Christine began her study of Koine Greek as a student at Geneva College. Her love for the language and desire to see her children fluent in the Greek of the New Testament inspired her to begin writing these lessons.

About Gerald R. McDermott

Gerald R. McDermott is Professor of Religion and Philosophy at Roanoke College in Salem, Virginia. He is the author of numerous books including *One Holy and Happy Society: The Public Theology of Jonathan Edwards* (Penn State Press), *Seeing God: Twelve Reliable Signs of True Spirituality* (InterVarsity), and *Cancer: A Medical and Spiritual Guide For Patients and Their Families* (Baker Books). He also serves as Teaching Minister at St. John Lutheran Church in Roanoke, Virginia.